Self-Discipline

Stop Procrastinating, Develop Daily Habits To Program Your Mind, Maximize Productivity And Achieve Your Goals

By

Damon Colmain

All trademarks and brands within this book are for clarifying purposes only and are the owned by the owners themselves, not affiliated with this document.

Table of contents

Chapter 1: Introduction

Self-discipline is just a way of progress. Lack of self-discipline is an essential cause of disappointment, dissatisfaction, underachievement, and unhappiness throughout life. It makes us rationalize and undercut ourselves.

Maybe the two greatest adversaries of success, happiness, and individual satisfaction are the Path of Least Resistance and the Expediency Factor.

The path of minimum resistance is what makes the individual easy in almost every situation. They look for alternate ways to everything. They show up at work at the last minute and leave at the first opportunity. They search for get-rich-quick schemes and pain-free income. After some time, they have developed the habit of looking for simpler and faster ways to get what they need instead of doing difficult but important things to make real progress.The Expediency Factor, an expansion of the law of least resistance, is surprisingly more terrible when driving individuals to failure and underachievement. This rule says, "Individuals perpetually look for the quickest and least demanding approach to get the things they need, at present, with next to zero worries for the longterm outcomes of their practices." at the end of the day, a great many people do what is convenient, what is fun and simple as opposed to what is vital for progress.

Every day, you will make the most sensible, hardest, and most important decision (for example, a messenger on the shoulder) or make fun, simple and almost zero value (for example, another person's demon) struggle shoulder). Every minute, if you want to be everything you want, you should win the expediency and win this battle, and oppose the formulation of the "lowest resistance path."

Assume Responsibility for Yourself

Another meaning of self-control is self-authority. Achievement is conceivable just when you can master your feelings, cravings, and tendencies. Individuals who cannot master their desires become powerless and dissolute, just as unreliable in different things.

Self- discipline can likewise be characterized as self-control. Your capacity to control yourself and your activities, control what you say and do, and guarantee that your behaviors are steady with your long-term objectives and goals is the superior person's mark.

Discipline has been characterized as self-denial. This requires that you deny yourself the simple delights. These temptations lead so many people astray. Instead, teach yourself to do just those things that you know are directly as long as possible appropriate for the moment.

Self- discipline requires delayed gratification, the ability to put off fulfillment in the present moment to enjoy greater rewards in the long term.

Think Long Term

Humanist Dr. Edward Banfield of Harvard University led a fifty-year study into the purposes behind upward financial portability in America. He inferred that the most important single quality of individuals who made incredible progress in life was a "long time perspective." Banfield characterized "time perspective" as "the amount of time an individual takes while thinking about deciding his current activities."

In other words, people with the most success are long-term thinkers. The scope of their investigation into the future can determine who they need to be and what they need to achieve. At that point, they then return to the present and decide the things that they should do—or not do—to accomplish their ideal prospects.

Long-term thinking applies to work, marriage, money, and individual conduct—every one of which is canvassed in the pages ahead. Successful individuals ensure that all that they do in the present moment is predictable with where they need to wind up in the long term. They practice self- discipline consistently.

Perhaps the most important word in long-term thinking is sacrifice. Successful people have the ability to throughout their lives make sacrifices in the short term, both large and small, to assure more excellent results and rewards in a long time.

Maybe the most important word in long-term thinking is sacrifice. Superior individuals have the capacity throughout their lives to make sacrifices in the short term, both large and small, to guarantee more remarkable outcomes and rewards in a long time.

You will see this ability to sacrifice because these people have spent a long time preparing, learning, and improving their skills to make themselves more valuable. This way, they can have a better life in the future, and no need to spend more energy socializing and enjoying their current life. Longfellow once stated: "Those heights by extraordinary men, won and kept, were not accomplished by flying. But, they were fully dedicated to working hard at night while their companions slept." Your capacity to think, plan, and work hard in the short term and train yourself to make the right decision before you do what is fun and simple is how to make a great future for yourself. Your capacity to think long term is a developed skill. As you improve on this, you will gradually be ready to predict with higher accuracy what might happen in the future due to your current behavior. This is the quality of an outstanding thinker.

Short-Term Gain Can Cause Long-Term Pain

There are 2 laws that you fall victim to when you neglect to rehearse self-control. The first is known as the "Law of Unintended Consequences." This law expresses that "the unintended results of an activity can be far more awful than the proposed outcomes of that conduct due to an absence of long-term thinking."

The second is the "Law of Perverse Consequences," which states that "a short-term action aimed at immediate gratification can lead to perverse, or the opposite, consequences from those at which it was aimed."

For instance, you may speculate time, money, or feeling with the craving and plan to be in an ideal situation and more joyful as a result. But since you acted without cautiously thinking, the results of your conduct ended up being far more regrettable than if you had done nothing by any means. Each individual has had this experience, and typically more than once.

Chapter 2: What Is Self-Discipline?

What is Self-Discipline? Self-control is the capacity to do what one needs to do to succeed, paying little mind to your emotional state. In life, it is one of the center ideals that empowers an individual to exceed expectations, or as Joseph Addison has said that "self-discipline is what, besides righteousness, really and raises one man over another." For example, a student who needs self-discipline will perform inadequately. Ability alone can't make a champion athlete; it requires a particular order of preparing to exceed expectations over every other person. In short, the virtues that an individual effectively develops inside themselves are the main drivers of all their prosperity. As it has been said that "we first make our habits, at that point our habits make us" (Cited in Franklin R. Bunch). William Feacher has noted that "if we don't discipline ourselves, the world will do it for us," which implies that if an individual doesn't train himself, he/she will surely flop throughout everyday life.

A student should consistently manage at the top of the priority list that self-control isn't inherent. It is 'temperance or obtained resource' (Duke Ellington). In other words, self-discipline is a habit.

 A habit in itself what the sages say 'we make our habits, then our habits make us' (Anonymous (Cited in Franklin R. Bunch). This implies it is the thing that a specific individual needs to get by customary preparing, and at whatever point a personal master it, it very well may be most priceless because it clears the path to all victories. Samuel Smiles gave a decent comment that:

- Sow an action, reap a habit;

- Sow a habit, reap a character;

- Sow a character, reap a destiny.

Sow Creating self-discipline is a self-conquering process, which is one of the most challenging assignments of all. Aristotle said that "I count him bolder who beats his wants than him who conquers his enemies; for the hardest triumph is over self." Before we start the mission of life working through forming self- discipline, we ought to comprehend its tendency. An individual who wishes to build up their self-discipline, in general, has to master the following characteristics.

They are:

- Self-Control,

- Motivation,

- Persistence,

- Goals,

- Will Power,

- Hard Work.

II. Factors of Self-Discipline

1. Self-Control

"Self-Control is characterized as internal resources with the ability to control/limit feelings, wants, actions, thoughts, words, and individual direction and change self's states and reactions—psychological, emotional, or conduct to the attractive heading that one wishes." (Baumeister, 2002; Baumeister and Exline, 2000; Logue, 1995). Self-control is generally settled from early in childhood.

When developed, this characteristic remains genuinely steady over one's lifetime and isn't influenced by increased age (Baumeister, 2002; Grasmick, Tittle, Bursick, and Arneklev, 1993; Strayhom, 2002).

Anyway, it tends to be exhausted after some time (Baumeister and Exline, 2000; Muraven, Tice, and Baumeister, 1998). It is comparable to a muscle, exhausted in the short run, yet reinforced with use after some time (Muraven and Baumeister, 2000; Muraven et al., 1999; Strayhorn, 2002).

An individual who can control her conduct is the person who can delay quick delight and seek after more significant standards, for example, in the completion of a college degree (Mischel, 1974; Strayhom, 2002). The idea of self-control is at the core of practically all regards in the life of youngsters and grown-ups. It is at the heart of liquor and substance abuse issues. If an individual has reliably practiced self-control, he/she will have the option to oppose the impulse to drink in overabundance. However, they are compelled by their companions. When one has mastered self-control, one is 'in charge of' one's brain and will just take part in one's preferred exercises and afterward to the degree that one wants. Suppose an individual lacks the self-control to the extent that they have become powerlessness over their desires. In that case, they will, in the long run, become captives of their wants.

Terri Moffit is a professor of Psychology and Neuroscience at Duke University who has led long term research with a group of 1,000 youngsters since birth. She has discovered that three components lead to accomplishment throughout everyday life: I.Q., family financial status, and self-control. Just one is anything but difficult to change, and that is self-control. A kid who has self-control at age four is bound to be happy and healthy as an adult. She inferred that the children with the strongest self-control ability among elementary school students and preschoolers are on the road to reduce medical problems and are most addicted to any substance in their 30s.

Self-control as a personality trait, although it is inside an individual, it is noticeable through their behavior. Self-control is measured in terms of the ability to delay gratification that has been considered an outcome of one's self-control (Strayhorn, 2002). The elements adding to self-control advancement occurs very early in adolescence through the socialization process (Brannigan, Gemmell, Pevalin, and Wade, 2002; Gottfredson and Hirschi, 1990; Grasmick et al., 1993). Family social factors including the family structure, parental degrees of hostility (Brannigan et al., 2002), parenting style (Arneklev, Grasmick, Tuttle, and Bursick, 1993), and methods of childhood socialization (Brannigan et al., 2002; Gottfredson and Hirschi, 1990) are among the factors adding to the advancement of self-control. Low degrees of self-control resulted in families in which guardians didn't closely monitor their kids' conduct. Theese families didn't perceive degenerate behavior when it happened and didn't punish the behavior if recognized (Arneklev et al., 1993; Gottfredson and Hirschi, 1990).

These socialization predecessors have been studied primarily in criminal behavior, where the idea and estimation of self-control were developed (Gottfredson and Hirschi, 1990). Gottfredson and Hirschi (1990), two pioneers of the field, have shown six self-control components. These six indicators of the lack of self-control are as follows:

- Impulsivity,

- Basic assignments,

- Risk-seeking,

- Physical activity,

- Self-centered,

- Temper (Arneklev et al., 1993; Barlow, 1991).

The first dimension of self-control – impulsivity – is a "tendency to respond to tangible stimuli in the immediate environment, to have a concrete 'here and now' orientation" (Gottfredson and Hirschi, 1990, p. 89). More significant impulsivity levels suggest an inclination to capitulate to immediate pleasurable satisfaction (Arneklev et al., 1993), a failure to delay gratification (Grasmick et al., 1993); therefore, a lower level of self-control. The primary variables of academic achievement are the individual's perseverance in performing tasks or considering impulse, simple tasks, and personal, interpersonal skills (self-centered, temperament).

The second dimension is called simple tasks (Barlow, 1991; Grasmick et al., 1993). It is the tendency to "lack diligence, tenacity, or persistence in the course of action . . . preferring easy or simple gratifications of desires" (Gottfredson and Hirschi, 1990, p. 89).

The third component of self-control is risk-seeking. It refers to the tendency "brave . . . inclining toward energizing, unsafe or exciting" activities (Gottfredson and Hirschi, 1990, p. 89). consistently seeking risk and pursuing excitement have lower levels of self-control (Barlow, 1991).

The fourth component of self-control refers to Individuals preferring physical activities to "psychological" or "mental" activities (an inclination for physical movement as indicated by Grasmick et al. (1993 tend to have low self-control (Gottfredson and Hirschi, 1990).

The fifth dimension of self-control is self-centered, which refers to the individual's tendency "to be self-centered, indifferent, or insensitive to others' suffering and needs" (Barlow, 1991; Grasmick et al., 1993).

The last component of the self-control scale is temper (Barlow, 1991; Grasmick et al., 1993).

People with low self-control "will, in general, have insignificant resilience for disappointment and little capacity to react to strife through verbal as opposed to physical signifies" (Gottfredson and Hirschi, 1990, p. 89).

What has been holding you back?

Before you can start thinking about improving your self-discipline, you need to ask yourself what has been keeping you down. This will give you a superior thought of your points of view, your convictions, your behaviors, and what move you can make to enable yourself to roll out positive improvements.

So here are a few questions I might want you to consider:

Why would you say you aren't as successful as you might want to be?

What convictions do you think have been sabotaging you? Also,

What behaviors do you think you could improve on?

Here are some other questions to consider?

Do you rationalize or delay?

Are you unclear and aren't sure of what you truly need?

Do you think you deserve these rewards, or would you say that you have inadvertently attacked your ability to achieve your goals?

Is there some piece of you that trusts you aren't fit?

Maybe all the above are excuses. This is the secret that makes a huge difference in your life. Stop making excuses. You can either have REASONS or RESULTS! Which one do you pick?

Is it true that you are sure about what you need?

Before we begin planning what moves we can make to move the right way, we should be sure about what that course is; therefore it is basic that you comprehend what achievement intends for you. Everybody has their meaning of accomplishment and it doesn't make you right or wrong. It is the thing that works for you and depends on your qualities. Is it about satisfying your desires, not somebody else's?

So here are 3 additional questions for you:

What does it mean for you to be successful? What does it look like?

Who are your role models when you consider achievement?

What attributes do your role models possess? Or what is it about them that makes them successful?

What does success mean to you?

Here are a few thoughts of what students have told me success intends to them:

Being ready to live in a particular manner, doing what you need to do

Being the individual, you need to be

Achieving the objectives you set for yourself

To be cheerful and settle for what you need and not for any less

Feeling fulfilled and satisfied

To arrive at success, does it imply that everything must be great? No, because success is about development and movement. It doesn't need to be static - it can change.

What does it take to be a successful individual?

Here are a few qualities I accept successful individuals will, in general, have

1. they are disciplined

2. they manage their time and actions effectively

3. long term thinkers and planners

4. willing to make sacrifices and delay gratification

5. invest in persistent learning

They make a habit of doing what unsuccessful individuals would prefer not to do.

Is it true that you are fit for embracing these characteristics? You are. You most likely do in areas you are successful in yet need to improve on in r areas you are still working on accomplishing. For instance - perhaps your accounts are immaculate because you spare and deal with your financial limit. Yet, your weight isn't perfect since you aren't putting time in reliably working out.

Self-discipline is necessary for success in order not to give in to temptations. And our two greatest temptations are:

the easy way out, and

the convenience factor.

It isn't our fault. We are altogether human, and they are our shortcomings. We should be disciplined enough to see past that and focus on RESULTS... in any case, all you have left are REASONS.

The uplifting news is you can accomplish practically any objective you set for yourself if you have self- discipline. The surprisingly better information is self-control can be educated.

If self-discipline is the way to progress, the absence of self-discipline is the way to disappointment. If self-discipline is the key to success, then the lack of self-discipline is the key to failure.

Why are habits important for making progress?

They say it takes 21 days to form a habit, so try to accomplish something every day, and after 21 days, it would be strange not to do so. It is your job to refuse to act in any other way than the good habits you are developing. You may not have thought of this; however, what do you think happens when you begin doing things that draw you nearer to making your progress? What do you think happens to your confidence?

When you finish what you set out to do - wouldn't you say you think you strengthen your trust with yourself?

- You will feel better about yourself

- You will feel more confident

- You will have more pride and self-respect

- You will most probably be willing to try more things since you have demonstrated how able and trained you genuinely are. As a general outcome, you wind up making more progress!

It sounds like a fair trade to me.

You can apply self-discipline in areas you want, including finances, relationships, health, work, family, and education.

Chapter 3: Five Steps To Help You Be More Disciplined

Decide and be sure about what you need. You should set reachable objectives.

Determine what price you are willing to pay that is, what habits are you ready to change? It's the negative behavior patterns in the way of self-control. Be explicit about what you will do any other form every day. Record it. Additionally, record your "what uncertainties" if you do wander.

Plan the day's activities ahead of time. If you're not used to planning, then start simple. The next night, record five things that you need to achieve the following day. At that point, the next morning marks them off as you do them - this is fundamental self-control. It's additionally framing new good habits and following advancement.

Resolve to be willing to pay the price. Make a move and do it, and

Finally, reward yourself for self-control accomplishments, yet ensure you pick rewards that help you push ahead and not go backward. Eg if you are attempting to get in shape, don't make food your premium.

Last tips:

I will leave with you some last tips that have helped me and of my students develop self-control:

- Model individuals who are already successful in the field you need to be effective in

- Be a deep-rooted student of your specialty - you can just improve. Try not to fall into the snare of accepting that you know it all since "you truly don't know what you don't have a clue."

- Put a plan set up to address temptations when they creep in because they will consistently sneak in and test you

- Draw on your successes. Consider what you have accomplished before to remind yourself how capable you are so that you don't lose your steam

- Put it in writing, and

- Take time to reflect daily. This is not a set and forget exercise

Chapter 4: Building Consistency And Discipline

You ought to acknowledge you have to have consistency in your activities, which encourages you to manufacture discipline, which causes you to accomplish your goal. So consistency and discipline do go inseparably.

You ought to likewise recognize the stuff for you to understand your ideal result. In this way, you need to exploit these ideas and thoughts and make an activity arrangement to arrive at your objective. Next, you need to make a variety of little achievements, which you ought to follow bit by bit day by day.

Start building and moving in the direction of your goal in little pieces. You don't get too overpowered along these lines, and it will give you some control over the errands you need to deal with. It is also an excellent way to avoid procrastination.

You must construct such discipline; you need to take progressive steps, day by day, and consistently keep up your ship's rudder.

If you need a better life, you need to settle on better choices and grow better and more grounded determination. You can't go around and blame others for your absence of results or bliss throughout everyday life.

Tips to Have and Increase Your Willpower

Have a powerful urge to accomplish a specific objective as self-discipline needs motivation and inspiration.

Remember that each incredible triumph requires extraordinary sacrifice. Accordingly, make sacrifices in the for time, effort, and challenging work.

Find mentors or good role models that push you upward. Furthermore, keep yourself responsible for bringing the best outcomes.

Have a plan to arrive, get away from what you need, and have a reasonable cutoff time set up. Be predictable with it and repeat all day, every day.

Discipline yourself to finish your activities until the end.

Build the habit of picking what is difficult and vital over what is fun and simple to do.

Take actions to make your objectives a reality since life changes just to the extent that you change.

Cultivate characteristics, for example, tolerance, perseverance, energy, tirelessness, mental fortitude, good faith, and enthusiasm for feeding your self-discipline.

Visualize your ideal results. Go about as though you were already successful

Keep going on if you experience disappointment and adversity. Face the difficulties throughout everyday life and endure them sufficiently long to succeed. Nobody else is going to ascend the stepping stool of achievement for you.

Create little achievements to build your willpower and push ahead by settling on choices that add to your targets.

Self-discipline is resolving to take the necessary steps, regardless of the difficulties and how hard it might be.

Use other's experience to better likely train yourself along your journey.

Get motivated and appreciate the process of keeping up an elevated level of self-restraint.

Do not blame, complain, or use excuses.

You must keep the fire burning. So, you could get motivation from books, from recordings, from individuals, from cites, from motion pictures, or a dream board. You could likewise discover inspiration by reading others' life stories and how they endure challenges on their approach to progress.

If I am telling you this, the massive catastrophe of life is that the vast majority, having no more expectation, surrender directly before achieving their objectives. They had now conquered the mountains, waters, hindrances, and dividers on their way, and all they required was a last advance around the bend to make it.

Tragically, directly before that turn, such a significant number of individuals surrender without even a moment's pause, without seeing how close they were. Consequently, figuring out how to build your self-discipline will help you cross that final stride to reach your long-awaited victory.

The Self Disciplined is Realistic

- Self-disciplined people have a negative attitude towards their perspectives and understand that instant joy may bring short-term satisfaction; however, it will cause frustration and disappointment in the long run. They have discovered that the things they want won't come automatically and have a detailed view of reality since useful things take difficult work. Their joy may be postponed as they work to accomplish this objective. Yet, their reasonable point of view eventually builds their odds of being cheerful over the long haul.

- They realize that to have the achievement, cash, and joy they want, they should set objectives and be propelled to oversee those objectives as far as possible, regardless of whether the end is more than a minute away.

The Self Disciplined Set Goals

- Self-taught individuals don't just wander through life, hoping to have achievement and satisfaction.

- They set objectives and are motivated to oversee those objectives to realization.

- When setting goals, they initially consider what they need to accomplish during their lifetime - or possibly at least 10 years from the present. Defining these long-term objectives helps structure an attitude that can be the base of every other choice.

- They make a rundown of littler objectives that will assist them with reaching their lifetime objective.

- They make an everyday daily agenda that encourages them to arrive at the achievement of their lifetime objective.

- They normally survey their daily agenda and plans to ensure they are steady with the objectives they are endeavoring to reach.

Self Disciplined are Motivated

- Self-disciplined individuals continually empower themselves. They don't insult themselves or discount their abilities. They converse with themselves with respect, persistence, and comprehension. This inspirational disposition keeps them spurred and not disheartened.

- They don't experience the day with a monotone rundown in their minds of things they need to achieve. They have an energy about what should be done, and their eagerness motivates them as far as possible. Much the same as a football coach wouldn't ordinarily request that his players dominate the match, a mythical person taught individuals to persuade themselves with enthusiasm and zeal, and that vitality makes them move.

- Self-disciplined individuals remain motivated by realizing how to feel great in any event when they are having an awful day. Everybody has days that make them need to creep into bed and never get out, yet disciplined individuals will persuade themselves by assuming responsibility for their musings and fulfilling themselves. They decide to run their mind positively.

Understand the Self Disciplined

Learning three things that self-disciplined individuals do makes it simpler to perceive how to show our own lives to act naturally trained. Self-trained individuals are sensible and realize that achievement, riches, and different things individuals take a stab at won't come naturally. They require difficult work, self-control, objective setting, and inspiration. Endeavor to be sensible, define goals, and be persuaded to achieve things. Oneself trained way of life will present the satisfaction and achievement you have always dreamed of having.

Self-discipline and qualities are characteristics we as a whole will in general battle with. We know the things we ought to do, and we know when we ought to do them; however, we are all very easily influenced when picking between the enjoyment things and the work things.

Thus, it is continuously a smart thought to structure your business around something that you appreciate doing. This way, work is play, and along these lines, it turns out to be pleasurable and straightforward to do everyday business tasks.

Self-made millionaires all have the craving and drive to consider themselves answerable for their prosperity. They all practice self-discipline.

They comprehend that self-discipline and stack-ability are their most significant single characteristics and weapons for progress, both throughout everyday life and for turning into an independent tycoon.

If you can train yourself to do what you ought to do, when you ought to do it, your prosperity is ensured regardless of whether you feel like it or not. Take care of business and stick with it. Trust me, the awards out of sight the errands.

The primary key to turning into an independent tycoon is a long time perspective combined with a capacity to delay satisfaction for the time being. To turn into an independent tycoon, you should set a long-term financial goal of turning out to be and accepting that you can become wealthy.

You need to discipline yourself every day and with every expenditure to guarantee that you do just those things that will at last assurance; you will accomplish your long-term objective.

Successful individuals pay the price that unsuccessful people will not pay. The contrast between successful individuals and unsuccessful individuals is that successful individuals have a propensity for doing the things that unsuccessful individuals won't and don't do!

Self-discipline implies self-authority, self-control, self-obligation, and self-bearing, and what are those things?

Simple, the things that failures don't like to do are the same things that successful people don't like to do either, yet successful individuals do them anyway because they understand that these are the costs that they should pay for the achievement that they want.

Successful individuals get stick ability. Stick ability is the glue that keeps you on the track to progress. Disappointments do not have the stick ability factor, so they tumble off the way before arriving at their goal.

Achievement is simple when you follow a framework. If a framework works and makes tycoons, at that point, it stands to detect that if you use a similar framework, at that point, the framework will work for you and your experience and enjoy the same outcome.

A typical example here would need to be McDonald's. Everybody on the planet knows McDonald's. Everybody also realizes that McDonald's doesn't make the best burgers globally, yet they are as yet the best burger franchise in the world.

The framework works. Presently, there is a little well-established certainty that only one out of every odd McDonald's franchisee is useful and valid! Indeed, even with McDonald's ~, not every person makes it. Why not, you may ask? Simple! They don't adhere to the rules, they don't follow the framework, and they don't have self-disciple.

Here are a few Success tips ~ For Entrepreneurs:

Successful individuals are progressively worried about satisfying outcomes.

Failures are more concerned with pleasing methods.

Unsuccessful people do things that are tension relieving.

Successful people do things that are goal-achieving.

Unsuccessful individuals, then again, like to do the things that are fun, simple, and which give immediate satisfaction.

Successful people do things that are important and necessary.

Every act of self-discipline enhances your other disciplines also.

Your self-esteem goes up every time you practice self-discipline, and you like and value yourself even more.

The more you exercise control in minor things, the more capable you become of the great discipline in the great opportunities and challenges of life.

Successful people never give up; they adapt, adjust, and have stick ability.

Keep in mind, everything in life is a test similar to when you were in school.

Regular, you discover some new information about yourself, your life, your reality. Every day, every hour, and sometimes each moment, you are stepping through an examination of self-dominance, self-control, and self-discipline.

The keys to self-discipline are simple. At the point when you focus on somebody, respect your commitment. If you focus on yourself, stay committed totally!

When you do break a commitment you made to yourself, understand that you are human. Organize your responsibilities that you make to yourself a similar way you do for other people.

With self-discipline comes dignity. You can't carry on with the life you want if you do not care for yourself.

Honor all parts of you:

Respect your body at the point when your body sends signals to focus on them. You are a structured masterpiece, and your body can let you know when something isn't quite right. Observe what your body says and give yourself the VIP treatment with the goal that you can be the most productive and most gainful you that you can be. Exercise, yoga, and so forth added to your day can help you balance your body and psyche.

Fill your mind with supporting, favorable, engaging information. Read books since learning can be a total pleasure. Have meaningful conversations with other people who have alternate points of view, backgrounds, philosophies, etc. Avoid malicious individuals, including negative discussions. As opposed to vegetating before the T.V., instead tune in to glad, positive music.

Remember your soul and respect it. You have to feel connected to something bigger than yourself. Reconnect with your Creator through prayer or even through isolation in nature. Locate a Bible-based church, expecting that you are of that conviction. Grant your soul to develop in quality and insignificance to you. At the point when you settle on choices, think about more significant benefits instead of prompt delight.

Try not to disregard your physical well-being. Self-discipline is essential, yet you should deal with your physical wellbeing. You can't achieve your expectations, dreams, objectives, and so on if your body isn't okay. Follow a solid eating routine. Try not to deny yourself legitimate rest and exercise. Keep your weight at a sound level. Try not to smoke. Don't over enjoy caffeine or liquor.

Respect your time. This implies you have to respect the time you spend at work, with your family, in play, and individual time. You have to have enough space in your life for these regions, so ensure that you plan time to invest alone and energy to go through with family similarly that you do regarding work and other significant duties.

When you add things to your written schedule, you prioritize you, and through self-discipline, you can keep to your priorities.

Self-discipline is crucial if you wish to live your life most fully and realize your goals. You must learn to control your emotions while making wise choices. This is one of the most positive things you can do for yourself. If you master the art of self-discipline, you will have the life you have always wanted. When you include something to your written plan, prioritize you and self-control, you can keep to your needs.

Self-discipline is essential if you wish to carry on with your life in the fullest manner and understand your goals. You should figure out how to control your driving forces while simultaneously settling on healthy choices since this is among the best things that anybody can accomplish for themselves. You can have the existence you have frequently needed if you get familiar with the craft of self-control.

Chapter 5: 6 Reasons Why Self Discipline Is Important For Success

Self-discipline is the way to achieve throughout everyday life. You can't prevail in existence without it. Fruitful individuals will consistently propose you to remain disciplined. In any case, the inquiry is "the reason self-control is significant for achievement throughout everyday life"?

Self-control causes you to become relentless power of vitality to arrive at the greatest level in your life. If you need to get fruitful throughout everyday life, the primary thing you have to do is teach yourself.

Let's get to know 6 Reasons Why Self Discipline Is Important For Success.

1. Self-discipline creates a habit.

Habits can make you or break you. Self-discipline makes a habit in your life that develops just through the order. Most people never stay restrained in their lives since they are lazy. However, laziness is a type of habit as well. Successful individuals teach themselves to work and remain reliable to it. Also, it turns into a habit. This is the thing that pulls in accomplishment in their lives.

2. It helps you get things done.

Self-discipline is important to get things done. It can be anything, whether you are committed to reading or completing tasks in a timetable. When teaching yourself to do all the work, you need to build a role around it. This habit makes you a successful person in life. Self-discipline is important to success because it keeps you stable in your daily life, and when you feel reliable, you will do whatever you need in your daily life.

3. It helps you to focus.

We live in a world full of distractions. Self-discipline allows you to focus on your goals. It will enable you to persist in completing the work required to make progress. At the point where the goal is the center, you will do all the work that should be done. An efficient individual has a keen focus. They constantly look forward to their goals and achievements in their daily lives. This encourages them to make extraordinary progress in life.

4. It boosts your self-esteem and work ethic.

Success comes from an individual who has confidence in himself and is the hardest person in the meeting room. Self-discipline encourages you to support your confidence and professional ethics. When you are self-study, you are improving your professional ethics by upholding your professional ethics. It will help you achieve your goals. In any case, when you complete your goals regularly, you will begin to support your confidence and trust in your work.

5. It helps you to achieve mastery.

Success comes to the individuals who are experts, not beginners. If you need achievement, you should be master something. You become master by putting the work and going through up to 10,000 hours on a particular something. Mastery accompanies discipline. A great many people fall flat since they don't master anything. Successful individuals do something and master it. Along these lines, this is how self-control will bring out dominance, and authority will bring out progress.

6. It helps you to become the best version of yourself.

Achievement is when you are worth it. You currently cannot have a successful personality. According to these principles, you need to upgrade every day.

You need to be your best form to be useful in your daily life. Self-control makes you develop day by day. When you accomplish something reliably, you become more and more commonplace. This is why self-control is essential to the progress and development of daily life.

Chapter 6: The Pathway To Self-Discipline

Considering that such an extensive amount of what we do regularly is propensity driven, building up the correct inclinations will help ingrain the perfect measure of control into our lives.

Yet, where do propensities originate from, and how are they created? What's more, for what reason is that when we attempt to change our inclinations by either getting out from under negative behavior patterns or building great propensities, we just finish for such a long time before we surrender and return to our old ways?

The most concerning issue, particularly with propensities that we've had for a considerable length of time and even decades, are the neural pathways that have been carved in our minds. Neural pathways help to interface up neural systems to play out a specific capacity, for example, strolling up the stairs, smoking a cigarette, or setting up some espresso with a particular goal in mind.

Neural pathways help to computerize conduct that is continually rehashed with an end goal to lessen cognizant preparing power in the psyche. This permits the mind to concentrate on different things that may be going on. This stems from our initial days as people and is a piece of our hereditary cosmetics, considering an increasingly proficient psyche that can be utilized towards numerous different things instead of the ordinary.

Notwithstanding, it's the alleged commonplace practices that are rehashed, which work to keep us down by and large. In general, we will have all the more negative behavior patterns unfavorable to our lives than great propensities that help push us ahead.

Considering that those neural pathways get carved further and more profound after some time, it gets increasingly hard to get out from under negative behavior patterns or even frame great ones when the awful ones disrupt the general flow.

In any case, if you can impart the accompanying propensities into your life, you'll see that restraining yourself gets far simpler. It won't occur incidentally. Recollect that propensities set aside some effort to shape and to break. In any case, on the off chance that you start little and manufacture, you won't be thinking about how you can teach yourself anymore since you'll typify the specific propensities that advance self-restraint throughout everyday life.

Gratitude

We invest to an extreme degree an excessive amount of energy needing things. The propensity for appreciation helps move us away from continually needing what we don't have and acknowledging what we do have. At the point when we do this, some great movements start to happen.

The impacts of appreciation are expansive. From improving our psychological wellness to our enthusiastic prosperity, and our otherworldliness, appreciation can accomplish such a great deal. It assists with moving us away from a condition of need and towards a state of bounty.

When we live in a condition of need, it turns out to be challenging to concentrate on being restrained and accomplishing our objectives. We spend such an extensive amount of our psychological limit on stressing over what we don't have and living in a dreadful condition that we disregard what we do have.

The condition of need converts into physical sicknesses. It produces pressure and discharges pressure hormones, for example, cortisol and epinephrine, which impact various frameworks in our body. When we stress, our stomach related, conceptive, and invulnerable frameworks are largely antagonistically influenced.

Go through 10 minutes, consistently working out all the things that you're appreciative of. Regardless of whether you believe you don't have anything to be thankful for, discover something. Look for, and you will find.

Forgiveness

When we spend a considerable part of our days in a condition of outrage, lament, or blame, we make a more significant number of issues than we make arrangements. Despise, and outrage expends unquestionably more vitality than affection and absolution. At the point when we excuse, we figure out how to relinquish certain things.

Without the propensity for pardoning, we were unable to accomplish self-restraint. We're too stressed over how somebody wronged us to spotlight discipline or achieve our objectives.

If somebody hurt you, figure out how to excuse them. It doesn't mean you need to overlook it. Simply pardon and discharge that negative vitality back into the universe.

By excusing, we let go of cynicism that destroys our capacity to act naturally restrained. If you need to figure out how to train yourself, pardoning is one significant road. While it probably won't appear to be a control propensity from the outset, it's one of the most significant ones that exist.

Consider all the individuals you're furious with or that have wronged you, and record why you excuse them. Attempt to imagine their perspective.

What might you have done in their circumstance? Attempt to discover some funniness in it. Attempt to find an exercise learned in all that unfolded.

I know firsthand precisely that it is so difficult to excuse a few people, particularly those that have genuinely wronged me throughout everyday life. In any case, it wasn't until I relinquished each one of those sentiments of hurt and ill will before things truly began to improve. I was so bustling, stressing, and focusing on that I wasn't generally pushing forward.

Meditation

Contemplation assists with comforting our psyches. It gives us otherworldly centeredness that goes about as a road of development. At the point when we ponder, we counterbalance the clamor, as it were, and understand that we're only one of a lot of associated creatures right now.

Contemplation likewise affects our capacity to act naturally restrained. It clears the psyche's palette and sets the correct tone for the afternoon. It helps improve our psychological, enthusiastic, physical, and profound well-being at the same time, permitting you to procure the absolute most outstanding outcomes for little time contributed.

Contemplation doesn't take long. It very well may be done in 10 or 15 minutes. Keep your psyche still, and don't allow it to meander. At the point when it begins to wander, reel it back. Feel your vitality grounded in the earth, open your palms to confront the sky, and truly feel the air as it moves all through your lungs.

Contemplation is tied in with adjusting our physical bodies to our profound or celestial bodies. When we can change the two, we can carry on with a progressively engaged life by not agonizing over the everyday things that will, in general, burden us. It assists with easing our burden.

Active Goal Setting

If you've tracked with my blog, you realize the amount I have confidence in a dynamic objective setting. This is not quite the same as a detached, objective setting. With inactive goal defining, you set objectives in your brain. They're detached because they need solid subtleties. You haven't appropriately characterized them, so they live in theory.

Dynamic objectives are extraordinary. With dynamic goals, they're worked out. They have significant importance. They're explicit and quantifiable. Furthermore, you have an arrangement for their accomplishment. When we set long haul objectives right now, we also participate in a dynamic objective setting every day; it's far simpler to accomplish our fantasies.

Dynamic objective setting ingrains discipline since it provides us guidance. It likewise encourages us to keep away from interruptions by observing what should be done in a given day. Without dynamic objectives, we're left similar to a boat without a sail stuck in stormy waters.

To set dynamic objectives, first, you should put some long haul objectives. On the off chance that you have long haul objectives, at that point, you have to take part in a month to month, week after week, and day by day objective setting and arranging. What's more, you likewise need to effectively keep tabs on your development towards your goals.

You can perceive how far you've come, where you are, and how far you've left to go with following and examination. It's far harder to get occupied because you can see the outcomes there directly in front of you. What's more, your intuitive psyche will discover fewer approaches to deceive you or assist you with concealing reality.

Each morning, make some day-by-day objectives for yourself, distinguish the most significant undertakings that should be done in the day, and pursue the frog afterward.

Eat Healthily

Many people don't understand that the human body spends enormous vitality preparing and processing nourishments (10-25% of it). When the eating regimen is wealthy in sugars, fats, and even proteins, the body is utilizing more vitality to process that nourishment, some of which is, to a great extent, futile to us.

Crude nourishment and organic products offer the most significant lift for vitality since they require less energy to process and give more vitality to use sometime later. This is otherwise called an upgraded Thermic Effect of Food (TEF) or Dietary Induced Thermogenesis (DIT).

The measure of vitality we have assumes an enormous job in how centered we are. At the point when we're engaged, we can move toward our objectives with discipline. At the point when we're excessively out cold from the nourishment that we've eaten, this is far harder to accomplish. We devote most of our energy to being too tired and unable to even consider accomplishing anything.

However, eating a hearty breakfast is critical to a good day. For this, you need to design dinner and end some negative behavior patterns. If you keep eating cheap food, you will not have the energy to eagerly move towards your goals or complete tasks. Nourishment can change the neurochemical cosmetics of the cerebrum and impacts the psyche body association. Decide on crude, sound, and natural nourishments when you can and limit your admission of garbage.

Sleep

Rest is straightforwardly associated with our capacity to teach ourselves. Also, getting the best possible measure of shuteye is an imperative essential to completing anything. When we don't get enough rest, it influences our mindset, capacity to center, judgment, eating routine, and general well-being.

When we talk about constant lack of sleep, the sort that influences numerous people, things deteriorate. Studies show that individuals who are denied the correct rest are at a more severe hazard for specific infections. The absence of rest significantly affects our invulnerable framework.

It's essential to get at any rate 6 hours of rest, regardless. Do whatever it takes not to drink an excessive amount of caffeine in any event 5 hours before sleep time with the goal that you don't interfere with your normal rest cycle. Avoid a disproportionate number of poisons for the day, for example, liquor, cigarettes, or doctor-prescribed medication, on the off chance that it very well may be evaded.

In general, the advantages of getting enough rest are sweeping. Besides helping you be increasingly taught, it will improve your memory, control irritation and agony and lower pressure. More rest will also prod your innovativeness, improve your evaluations, hone your consideration, maintain a strategic distance from misery, and breakpoint your odds for mishaps.

Exercise

Exercise is a cornerstone propensity. It goes about as a foundation to a real existence loaded up with significant and positive inclinations and liberated from negative behavior patterns. Need to know how you can genuinely teach yourself? Impart the cornerstone propensity for practice into your morning schedule.

I can't start to communicate the advantages of activity. I've discussed a few posts and books that I've composed. Be that as it may, on the other hand, numerous individuals extoll the extraordinary advantages of activity. However, not every person focuses on practice in their lives. So why not?

While numerous individuals are caught up going around, attempting to complete things in the day, they're neglecting to take the bull by the horn when they don't work out. Numerous individuals imagine that they can't develop this propensity or have an excessive amount to do to stress over instead of working out. That is the place numerous individuals aren't right.

By ingraining the cornerstone propensity for work out, not exclusively would you turn out to be progressively restrained; however, you can improve your life in various manners. Practice decreases your degrees of stress and agony by discharging endorphins and synapses, for example, dopamine and serotonin.

Second, practice improves well-being by expanding the bloodstream and oxygenation of the body's cells, assisting with fending off ailments and lifting the safe framework. What's more, practice expands our capacity to concentrate on the primary job, permitting us to lead an increasingly taught life.

To ingrain the propensity for practice in your life, start little. Start by strolling around the square for 5 minutes toward the beginning of the day. Only 5 minutes. Do that for multi-week. At that point, increment it to 10 minutes and do that for seven days. Furthermore, proceed with this example. In the long run, exercise will turn into an all-out propensity.

Organization

To act naturally taught and accomplish our objectives, we should be composed. Association is a propensity that should be wholly typified, in your expert life, yet additionally in your own life. This incorporates sorting out the things in your home and office alongside the items in your psyche.

A sorted out life is a taught life. Start little on the off chance that you name yourself as totally dissipated. Start by arranging one small space every day. For instance, start by sorting out your work area cabinet. The following day, move onto setting your medication bureau in your washroom. Etc.

Do one little thing daily to improve your association. That is everything necessary.

Like the various propensities, the propensity for association can be gradually developed after some time. It requires some exertion and consideration; indeed, it will pay off massively over the long haul. At the point when the physical space around you is sorted out, your psyche turns out to be increasingly loose, calm, and ready to center.

Like this, you can be increasingly self-taught when your life is progressively composed. This incorporates keeping records alongside sorting out your drawers. At the point when you're finished utilizing something, set it back into where it has a place as opposed to simply forgetting about it.

It's the easily overlooked details that we do regularly that mainly affect the nature of our lives. Focus on the little stuff, and you'll receive enormous rewards.

Time Management

The vast majority that realizes me that I'm a significant defender of time the executives.

At the point when you're running 5 separate organizations, you nearly must choose the option to viably deal with your time. Without the propensity for the time the board, it would be incomprehensible for me to complete anything.

When we can appropriately deal with our time, we have space for the stuff that issues. In particular, we have room for the exercises that will assist us in accomplishing our objectives. To achieve our long haul objectives, we need to perform activities that probably won't be dire yet are unquestionably significant.

In time the executives, consider this the Not Urgent; however, an Important quadrant of exercises, otherwise called Quadrant 2. Nonetheless, the vast majority invest their energy with the Not Urgent and Not Important practices, otherwise called Quadrant 4. Otherwise called the time-squanderers.

If, our capacity for self-restraint is generally gotten from our ability to viably deal with our time. The noticeable time chiefs of the world are additionally the absolute best individuals in their separate fields. Why? Since they use time as an advantage instead of a depreciator.

Persistence

No arrangement of order propensities would be finished without determination. Diligence is a sure propensity that encourages us to not surrender. In any event, when we do come up short, it permits us to get back up once more. Without the propensity for diligence, self-restraint would be, to a great extent, unthinkable.

Why? Since accomplishing our objectives is difficult. Getting disheartened is simple. What's more, surrendering requires far less exertion than proceeding to push through, particularly towards something that delivers a great deal of torment before it gives us any joy.

Be that as it may, that is precisely the stuff. We have to understand that even the most well-known individuals prevailing in life have bombed many occasions over.

Disappointment is a significant venturing stone throughout everyday life. Without fizzling and bombing huge, we could not accomplish the grand objectives that we set for ourselves.

There are positively numerous approaches to impart this propensity; however, the most ideal path is to honestly think of some significant reasons for why you need the things in life. At the point when our senses are sufficient, they can get us through pretty much anything.

Chapter 7: Self-Discipline And Goals

The Seven-Step Method to Achieving Your Goals

There are seven fundamental advances that you can follow to set and accomplish your objectives quicker. There are increasingly unpredictable and definite goal-accomplishing philosophies. Yet, this Seven-Step Method will empower you to achieve multiple times more than you have ever achieved previously, and you will do as such far quicker than you can as of now envision.

Stage 1: Decide Exactly What You Want. Be explicit. If you need to increase your income, settle on a particular measure of cash instead of simply "get more cash-flow."

Step 2: Write It Down. An objective that isn't recorded as a hard copy resembles tobacco smoke: It floats away and vanishes. It is unclear and pitiful. It has no power, impact, or force. In any case, a composed objective becomes something that you can see, contact, read, and adjust if essential.

Stage 3: Set a Deadline for Your Goal. Pick a sensible timespan and record the date when you need to accomplish it. If it is a broad enough objective, set the last cutoff time and set sub deadlines or break ventures between where you are today and where you need to be later on.

A deadline fills in as a "driving framework" in your brain. The brain works quickly and effectively when you have concluded that you need to accomplish an objective by a particular time.

The rule is, "There is no such thing as unrealistic goals; there are only unrealistic deadlines." What do you do if you do not achieve your goal by your deadline?. You set another deadline.

A deadline is just a "guesstimate." Sometimes you will complete your goals before the deadline; sometimes, you will meet your goals before the deadline; in some cases, you will achieve your goals before the deadline, and sometimes you will achieve your plans after the deadline. When you set your goal, it will be inside the setting of a specific external conditions arrangement. If these conditions may change, making you change your cutoff time too.

Stage 4: Make a List of Everything You Can Think of That You Could Possibly Do to Achieve Your Goal. As Henry Ford stated, "The greatest objective can be cultivated if you simply separate it into enough little advances."

Make a list of the hindrances and challenges you, both external and internal, accomplish your objective.

Make a list of the extra information and abilities that you will require to accomplish your objective.

Make a list of the individuals whose collaboration and bolster you will require to accomplish your objective.

Make a list of all the things you can think about that you should do, and afterward add to this list as new errands and obligations happen to you. Continue composing until your list is finished.

Stage 5: Organize Your List by Both Sequence and Priority. A list of exercises sorted out by arrangement necessitates that you choose what you have to do first, what you have to do second, and what you have to do later on. Furthermore, a list sorted out by need empowers you to figure out what is increasingly significant and less significant. Here and their arrangement and need are the equivalents, yet frequently they are not.

For instance, what is most significant is your capacity to build up a field-tested strategy because of complete statistical surveying that you can use to accumulate the assets you require and start the business you have at the top of the priority list.

Stage 6: Take Action on Your Plan Immediately. Venture out—at that point, the subsequent advance and the third step. Get moving. Get going. Hurry. Try not to delay. Keep in mind: Procrastination isn't just the hoodlum of time; it is the criminal of life.

The contrast among victories and disappointments in life is essential that champs venture out. They are activities situated. As they said in Star Trek, they "go strikingly where no man has ever gone previously." Winners are happy to make a move without any assurances of progress. Although they're willing to confront disappointment and disillusionment, they're continually ready to make a move.

Stage 7: Do Something Every Day That Moves You in the Direction of Your Major Goal. This is the crucial advance that will ensure your prosperity: Do something, seven days per week, 365 days per year. Do whatever moves you, in any event, one bit nearer to the objective that is generally essential to you around then. At the point when you accomplish something consistently that moves you toward your objective, you create energy. This force, this feeling of forwarding movement, propels, rouses, and empowers you. As you create energy, you will discover it progressively simple to step toward your objective. Right away by any means, you will have built up the control of defining and accomplishing your goals. It will before long become simple and programmed. Before long, you will build up the propensity and the control of moving in the direction of your objectives always.

THE TEN-GOAL EXERCISE

This is one of the most remarkable objective accomplishing strategies I have ever found. I show it everywhere throughout the world, and I practice it myself consistently. Take out a spotless piece of paper. At the highest point of the page, compose "Objectives" and the current date. At that point, teach yourself to record ten objectives that you'd prefer to achieve in the following year. Write down financial, family goals, fitness goals, and goals for personal possessions, like a car or house. Don't worry about how you are going to accomplish these goals. Just write them down as fast as you can. You can write as many as 15 goals if you like; however, this exercise requires that you write down a minimum of ten within three to five minutes.

Select One Goal

Once you have written out your goals, imagine for the moment that you can achieve all of the goals on your list if you want them long enough and hard enough. Additionally, envision that you have an "enchantment wand" that you can wave to empower you to accomplish any one goal on your list inside twenty-four hours.

If you could accomplish any one goal on your list inside twenty-four hours, which one would have the best positive effect on your life at this moment? Which one goal would improve or change your life more than anything else?

If you somehow happened to accomplish it, which one goal would help you achieve a more generous amount of your different goals than all else? Whatever your response to this question, put a hover around this objective and afterward compose it at the highest point of a spotless piece of paper.

This objective, at that point, turns into your "Major Definite Purpose." It turns into your point of convergence and the arranging standard of your future exercises.

Make a Plan

Once you have worked out this goal, plainly and explicitly, and made it quantifiable, set a deadline time on your objective. Your intuitive brain needs a deadline with the goal that it can center and focus all your psychological powers on goal achievement.

Make a list of everything that you to can think about that you could do to accomplish your goal. Sort out this list by grouping and need.

Select the most critical or intelligent following stage in your arrangement and make a move on it right away. Venture out. Accomplish something. Do anything.

Make plans to take a shot at this objective every day until it is accomplished. From this minute forward, undoubtedly, "Disappointment isn't an alternative." Once you have determined that the goal can positively impact your life and set it as the decisive cause, please ensure that you will work towards the goal for as long as possible and do your best. You will never surrender until it is finished. This choice alone can transform you.

Use "Mindstorming" to Get Started

Here is another procedure you can use to significantly improve the probability that you will accomplish your most significant goal. This is the most unique innovative reasoning method I have ever observed.

More individuals have become well off utilizing this technique than some other way. Take another perfect piece of paper. Work out your Major Definite Purpose at the highest point of the page as an inquiry. At that point, teach yourself to compose at least twenty responses to the question.

For instance, if you will likely acquire a specific measure of cash by a particular date, you would compose the inquiry as, "How might I gain $XXX by this particular date?" You, at that point, train yourself to produce twenty solutions to your question.

This activity of "mind storming" will activate your mind, unleash your creativity, and give you ideas that you may never have thought of before. The following five will be troublesome, and the last ten answers will be more earnestly than you can envision, at any rate, the first occasion when you do this activity.

Regardless, you should apply your order and self-discipline to persevere until you have recorded in any event twenty answers. When you have produced twenty solutions, investigate your rundown and select one of those responses to make a move on right away. It appears that when you make a move on a solitary thought on your rundown, it triggers more thoughts and propels you to make a move on significantly a more significant amount of these answers.

The Great Law of Cause and Effect

The most significant utilization of the law of circumstances and logical results is that "contemplations are causes, and conditions are impacts." Your musings make a great state. At the point when you change your reasoning, you transform you. Your external world turns into an identical representation impression of your inward world.

Maybe the best revelation throughout the entire existence of thought is that "you become your opinion of more often than not." Moreover, the educator John Boyle stated, "Whatever you can consider on a proceeding with the premise, you can have."

Napoleon Hill, creator of the achievement exemplary Think and Grow Rich—which was first distributed in 1939, is as yet selling today—stated, "Whatever the psyche of man can imagine and accept, it can accomplish." When you consider your objective persistently and work on it consistently, increasingly, more of your psychological assets will be focused on pushing you toward that objective—and moving you toward that objective—and pushing your goal toward you. The order of the day by day objective setting will make you a ground-breaking, deliberate, and compelling individual. You will create confidence, self-assurance, and dignity. As you feel yourself pushing toward your objectives quicker and quicker, you will, at last, become relentless. In the following section, I will clarify how the utilization of self-control to create individual greatness is the most impressive advance you can take to accomplish all your material and enthusiastic objectives.

Activity Exercises:

Resolve today to "switch on" your prosperity system and open your goal-achieving component by choosing precisely what you genuinely need throughout everyday life.

Make a rundown of ten objectives that you need to accomplish within a reasonable time-frame. Record them in the current state, as though you have just completed them.

Select the one objective that could have the best positive effect on your life if you somehow managed to accomplish it, and record it at the highest point of another bit of paper.

Make a rundown of all that you could do to accomplish this objective, sort out it by arrangement and need, and afterward make a move on it right away.

Work on mind storming by working out twenty thoughts that could help you accomplish your most significant objective and then make a move on at any rate one of those thoughts.

Make plans to do something consistently, seven days every week, to accomplish your most significant objective until you are effective.

Consistently advise yourself that "disappointment isn't an alternative." No issue what, make plans to persevere until you succeed.

Chapter 8: Step By Step Instructions To Achieve Your Goals - A Simple Guide To Help You Get What You Want

One of the most satisfying things right now when we can accomplish our goals and carry on with the life we wanted. If that goal is at the top of the priority list that you have been considering for such a long time yet, you never had begun or achieved it, here is a guide that will help you figure out how to accomplish your goals.

- Decide what you need to accomplish. This will define your goals throughout everyday life. Make your goals specific and pick goals that are attainable or reasonable. One most ideal way to assist you with centering and accomplishing your goals is to carefully record it.

If you have a major goal as the main priority, break it down to smaller ones to see how you will advance on accomplishing your goals. If you need to shed 20 pounds in a half year, you should break it into losing 3 to 4 pounds every month, which would seem achievable.

- Believe in yourself and remain positive about life. Regardless of what many individuals say, you can't do it; you should trust you can. Feel that the sky is the limit if you accept. An uplifting mentality will assist you with continuing moving and, without a doubt, will open more doors on the most proficient method to accomplish your goals.

- Condition your mind and your subconscious about your goal as a main priority. Our mind wanders in inspiring us to do what we ought to, and the more we train our mind to 'see' what we need, the more it will pull in our goals, wants, and yearnings. Perception is an amazing asset that will likewise assist you with remaining submitted on accomplishing your goals.

- Set a need. If you have a few goals at the top of the priority list, set needs on which one you will handle first. This will assist you with remaining concentrated on each goal in turn and not being diverted by such huge numbers of things you need to accomplish, which will, in all probability, end in disorganization.

- Set a time frame by which you need to accomplish your goals. This will assist you with moving, and this will likewise propel you to get going. When you are finished with one goal, you can generally hop to another.

- Plan how you will work on your goals. Make a plan on the most proficient method to accomplish those goals by listing down activities that you have to do. If your transient goal is shed 4 pounds every month, you may most likely need to get rid of soda, or you should reduce the number of times you eat out in fast food, or you might need to take on a cardio practice or get included into sports.

- Identify your strengths and weaknesses. Decide your limitations. Discover resources that will assist you in building up your skills and abilities. Don't merely settle for what you know; continue learning.

- Take action. Work on your goals. Give time to work away at it ordinary and remain glad. Love what you are doing. You will discover satisfaction at last that you have dealt with your goals without denying yourself of joy.

- Celebrate your success. If you can achieve your goals, perceive that you have sure gone far and achieved something, so appreciate it.

It isn't sufficient to realize how to accomplish your objectives throughout everyday life. A goal will possibly stay a desire if you don't make a move on it. So start now.

14 Quick Tips for Achieving Your Goals

Every individual would dream of achieving the status of Bill Gates, Steve Jobs, and Warren Buffet. Nonetheless, numerous individuals simply restrict themselves with their dreams.

Accomplishing your goals needs something more than that. An additional edge is a thing that required being successful throughout everyday life.

Here are some of the tips:

- Have a long term goal.

- Set a time to achieve the goal.

- Break down your vision in too many numbers of smaller goals.

- Now set a definite time frame to achieve all the smaller goals.

- Continuously track down your improvement.

- Do not shut down on confronting disappointment.

- Learn from the mistakes.

- If you pass up a major opportunity to accomplish any of your short-term goals, attempt to address the mix-ups you have done and concentrate on achieving it.

- Never relax, and do not think that you have attained flawlessness.

- Select a well-known personality and select them as your good example.

- Try to inspire from their activities and seek to accomplish the goals.

- Imagine and picture your success, although you have not accomplished it.

- Try to motivate others through your activities.

- Keep motivating yourself and self-dependent.

- It is strongly recommended to have a positive attitude, which will trigger your enthusiasm.

- Picturing every one of your activities and accomplishing success in thoughts are the first few steps to be done to achieve your goal.

The question is, would you like to accomplish your ultimate goal?

Chapter 9: Self-Control Benefits And Importance

Self-control is one of the most significant aptitudes everybody ought to have. This expertise is essential in each everyday issue, and however, the vast majority recognize its significance, not very many plan something to reinforce it. As opposed to regular conviction, self-restraint doesn't mean being brutal toward yourself or carrying on with a constrained, prohibitive way of life. Self-control implies poise, which indicates inward quality and control of yourself, your responses, and your activities.

Self-control enables you to stick to your choices and complete them without adjusting your perspective, which is an essential prerequisite for achieving your goals.

Ownership of this feature allows you to continue to choose and plan until the choice is made. Besides, it also manifests as an internal quality that can help you overcome addiction, delay, and indifference and accomplish everything you do. Willpower and Self Discipline Want to Move from Words to Action?

Fortify your determination and self-control!

Determination and self-control are breakthrough motors that can provide you with inner unity to achieve whatever you need to do. One of its fundamental characteristics is the ability to eliminate instant satisfaction and pleasure, and there are some noteworthy additions, which require investment and energy to obtain.

Self-discipline is one of the critical factors of progress. It communicates in many ways: OK. The ability not to yield even after disappointment and failure. The ability to resist distraction or temptation.

Keep trying until you achieve what you plan to do. Life brings difficulties and problems to progress and achievement. To transcend these difficulties and problems, you need to act diligently and perseverance, which requires self-control. The ownership of this aptitude prompts confidence and fearlessness, and thus, to joy and fulfillment. Then again, the absence of self-restraint prompts disappointment, misfortune, wellbeing, and connections' issues, heftiness, and different issues.

This expertise is additionally valuable for defeating dietary problems, addictions, drinking, smoking, and negative propensities. You also need it to cause yourself to sit and contemplate, practice your body, grow new abilities, and personal development, profound development, and reflection. As said before, many people recognize the significance and advantages of self-restraint; however, not very many find a way to create and fortify it. Notwithstanding, you can reinforce this capacity like some other aptitude. This is done through activities and preparing, which can discover at this site.

Self-discipline helps you:

- Avoid acting rashly and on impulse.

- Fulfill promises you make to yourself and others.

- Overcome procrastination and laziness.

- Keep working on a project, even after the initial rush of enthusiasm has faded away.

- Go to the gym, swim or walk, even if your mind tells you to stay at home and watch Television.

- Continue working on your diet and resisting the temptation of eating fast foods.

- Wake early in the morning.

- Meditate regularly.

- Overcome the habit of watching too much TV.

- Start reading a book, and read it to the last page.

- It will be much easy for you to strengthen your self-discipline if you:

Understand its significance in your life.

- Be aware of your undisciplined behavior and its consequences. As this awareness increases, you will become more convinced that you need to change your life. Regardless of procrastination, laziness, or the effort to give up and stop what you are doing, try to act and act according to your own decisions. You can use special simple exercises to enhance your self-discipline ability; even if your current ability is weak, you can practice anytime, anywhere. Although gradually becoming self-training is not easy because it often conflicts with our quick needs and motivation, it is feasible. Here are several ways to gradually train yourself: **Be educated:** Don't bounce into accomplishing a significant objective without doing your exploration. While you might be energized and anxious to begin; by understanding the stuff to be effective and the means expected to arrive.

- **Avoid naming yourself:** We all have that voice in the rear of our head that rehashes a wide range of nonconstructive data. If your voice is revealing to you things like "That is simply not 'you;'" or "you're simply not the sort to prevail at that objective," – it is basic that you learn and practice an increasingly positive anecdote about yourself.

- **Don't put your life on pause:** Sure, it's smarter to go to that large gathering, wedding, or other significant occasions when you are putting your best self forward. Be that as it may, don't make living dependent upon satisfying the entirety of your objectives. Continue endeavoring toward accomplishing them, however, make a mind-blowing most meanwhile.

- **Consider the planning:** Be aware of the planning in which you need to practice restraint progressively, on the off chance that specific seasons are additional testing (i.e., for some, the special seasons are not the best time to start well-being and wellness plans), center around a progressively reasonable period.

- **Don't beat yourself up for saw disappointments and misfortunes:** As you are on your excursion toward better control, there will be incidental difficulties. Try not to think about them as disappointments that characterize your whole endeavors at personal growth. The entirety of your difficult work so far isn't represented by one set-back today. Pardon yourself and get back to the program.

- **Identify your short-and long haul objectives — and be explicit:** Simply expressing "I will be increasingly taught by the way I manage my accounts," or "I will turn out to be progressively fit," won't cut it. You have to work out the particular objectives en route and to show such goals in a spot where you will see them every day — like on a significant bit of paper in on your kitchen divider.

- **Choose objectives directly for you;** don't surrender to others' desires: How you accomplish poise benefits is needy upon your objectives, capacities, and inspiration. Pick targets that are significant to you.

- **Aim for sensible objectives:** A definite method to fall flat at accomplishing restraint targets is by picking unattainable objectives. If you've never run, a long-distance race presumably isn't in your not so distant future. Practical goals are fundamental to progress.

- **Don't try too hard:** As you are energetically plunging forward with your new poise program, if you notice that it's wearing you out or hindering different parts of your life, you might be trying too hard. It is imperative to register with yourself normally to ensure everything is on target.

- **Self-screen your advancement:** Self-observing methods keeping a predictable record of your improvement. Therapists frequently incorporate self-observing as a component of intercession programs to gather information, yet additionally, because it is identified with improved consistency with program targets. How you screen your advancement is up to you (i.e., could be on your telephone, your PC, or a bit of paper); interestingly, you do it.

- **Share your arrangement with a companion:** By imparting your new poise destinations to other people, you will be bound to stay with them.

- **Seek help varying:** If your arrangement demonstrates exceedingly dubious because something is blocking or disrupting your advancement, it might be an excellent opportunity to request assistance from a companion or expert.

- **Be hopeful; picture your ultimate objective:** It appears glaringly evident, yet by continually envisioning yourself in a positive light and having a playful mentality, you will be bound to succeed.

- **Take breaks:** Sometimes, another self-control approach can get overpowering and will make the individual feel denied. By giving yourself sensible breaks (i.e., an individual attempting to shed pounds may permit one day seven days in which the requests are less stringent), you will be less inclined to surrender out and out.

- **Practice self-care:** While you might be doing extraordinary toward accomplishing your objectives, make sure to deal with yourself in different territories so you stay balanced and solid.

- **Don't make new issues:** Becoming progressively taught ought not to include nonsensically costly projects, nourishments, specialists, classes, and so forth. For instance, people endeavoring to accomplish New Year's goals may eat a wide range of undesirable nourishments during the special seasons, just to be trailed by excessively costly sound food sources after the new year (Pope, Hanks, and Just et al., 2014).

- **Reward yourself:** Don't neglect to remunerate yourself en route. Little, yet significant, rewards help look after inspiration.

- **Identify good positive examples**: As you adventure toward your goal, know about people who either move or damage your endeavors by their practices. Stick with the main gathering.

- **Avoid interruptions and allurements:** Along with timing, endeavors at restraint are improved when you are not exposed to conditions that meddle with your advancement (i.e., a kitchen brimming with low-quality nourishment won't help somebody moving in the direction of good dieting).

- **Adjust objectives, however, just as vital:** If you are finding that your unique goals were either too difficult to even think about being practically met or not testing enough, it's alright to change them.

- •**Share your victories:** As you end up doing great with your arrangement, share your advancement with other people who will be glad for you. This will upgrade your confidence and proceeded with inspiration.

- **Be in for the long stretch:** Remember, turning out to be progressively self-taught might be another mentality for you; and attitudes can be hard to change. Changing our practices and desires is continually testing, and rewards set aside some effort to figure it out. However, if you stay with it while likewise encircling your objectives as a way of life (instead of brief) transforms, you will be bound to get results.

Chapter 10: Procrastination; The Silent Killer Of Dreams

I saw a man who looks exactly like a shadow, holding a killer weapon. He wanders about the globe, trying to kill the dreams of many. His body was marked a SILENT KILLER, and he works quietly; however, it hurts perilously. This man has destroyed many people's dreams who failed to notice and acknowledge his essence and the individuals who appear not to be disturbed by his presence. Although he passes them by to the individuals who remained in awareness and prepared to deal with the silent killer. Many have become victims of this silent killer, whose real name is Mr. Procrastination. You need to be aware in other to be an exception.

WHAT IS or instead WHO IS Mr. PROCRASTINATION?

Procrastination refers to moving of occasions or activities inconclusively. When an individual continues postponing what he is supposed to do now into the future, he is procrastinating.

Procrastination is a delay in an obligation's performance, probably because you would prefer not to do it or have no eager doing it. Life isn't about what we like to do, but things that need to be done. Perhaps you dislike getting up promptly in the morning to get ready for work, yet you need to do it since you must go out in time.

Individuals talk progressively about plans and objectives without much reference to Mr. Procrastination as regards to life achievement.

Some people have incredible vision and grand plans to achieve their goals, but procrastination has become the silent killer of dreams. As the years go by, they have little or no achievement. I firmly believe that everyone can be enriched by nature in various ways.

We need to cheer up, starting today, to prevent delays from ruining our dreams. Some people have made it in life from nothing, which is because they began promptly without relenting. They will not give procrastination a chance in their life pursuit.

Procrastination kills a man's dream because many people have not come to understand this as one of the impediments standing against their advancement. It is the point at which a man recognizes that he can seek an answer; procrastination is a significant yet quiet hindrance to a man's prosperity because it steals time. Time is perhaps the best resource given to man by God and necessitates appropriate use for its augmentation. This is why it is vital to express the time an objective is relied upon to be acknowledged when defining a purpose. This gives a push as your time begins ticking from the minute you set your goal.

How about people who have no objective? The terror procrastination unleashes on an individual with no stated goals is more. The fear procrastination releases on a person with no expressed purposes are more. They have not allowed the time factor to give them a push. They approve of their wishes while the time passes quickly away from them.

Additionally, if not handled in a man's life, procrastination will leave him with the existence of emptiness. It will be a thing of delight and self-satisfaction for a retired man to think back in his years and grin on tallying his impressions. A man without any accomplishments throughout his life can not encounter a pleasant feeling of self-satisfaction. Procrastination can prevent you from securing the economic and social benefits of life. It can lead to feelings of guilt, depression, and lack of self-confidence.

It can kill a man's dream by causing him to lose good opportunities in life. Luck has been characterized as when preparation meets opportunity. One should be prepared in other to grab hold of the opportunities life exhibits in other to achieve success out of it. If you procrastinate, you will not be able to get prepared to take advantage of life opportunities.

Prod Yourself Out of Procrastination

Have you, at any point, thought about how to overcome procrastination? It is imperative to learn if you repeatedly wind up stuck in an unhealthy body, intimate relationship, friendship, or workplace.

I had a customer who remained in a toxic workplace inspired by a paranoid fear of dismissal and disappointing others to the point of enduring torment for over six years. Researcher, Joseph R. Ferrari of DePaul University, said there are three fundamental types of procrastinators:

- Arousal procrastinators: They love the thrill of last-minute projects and work.

- Decisional procrastinators: They become frozen by fear and anxiety.

- Avoidance procrastinators: They have a habit of putting off challenging or monotonous tasks.

Below are some tips:

1. When high anxiety or fear is included, seek help to find and crumple the impact of a potential past traumatic event.

2. If you procrastinate because you tend to keep away from troublesome people or stay away from the experience of being rejected, learn some positive self-talk. For example, say this to yourself, "They are rejecting the idea, not me."

3. When feeling overpowered by a task's enormity, whether it is moving from home or composing a book, break the assignment into little steps, called chunking.

4. If you procrastinate because the undertaking or task is depleting, compensate yourself a while later or do a piece of the depleting task and afterward carry out certain responsibilities that stimulate. If your job expects you to do exercises that debilitate and deplete you, look for opportunities to assign, change careers, or volunteer to do tasks that use your strength. When we engage in tasks that utilize our strengths, we are in the zone, and time flies.

5. To handle perfectionism, start to observe and value the benefit of taking risks and making errors. Build up a mantra for when mix-ups happen, such as, "Another mistake another life lesson!"

6. Learn the difference between excellence and perfection. Tell yourself, "It is good enough" for tasks that do not require total accuracy. Do some activities just for fun.

7. Be clear about your needs. We regularly mistakenly think we are procrastinating when we decide to set work aside to put work aside and listen to a hurting co-worker. I once heard a dad state, "I don't get why it takes you so much time to put the kids to bed. I do it in a short time." How long does it take to put a child to bed, comfort a hurting friend, or sort out a spat between kins?

The answer can not be answered in clock time. When the child is settled, the friend feels calm, and when the children have made an agreement.

How to Deal With Procrastination

Procrastination maintains a strategic distance from or postponing essential activities and tasks for work with a lesser significance level. Procrastination isn't just a time squanderer; it also destroys deadline management and ruin productivity.

To adapt to procrastination is getting over the lethargic-self. When the explanation behind procrastination can be distinguished, there are approaches to fix it as well. In many cases, we see ourselves doing the following things:

1.   We take out our laptops to do an essential task and then just leave to brew a cup of coffee or make tea.

2.   When we start, the telephone rings, and we tend to speak for longer than required, killing maximum minutes.

3.   When we are just about to start our work, we end up going on a social networking website or checking our emails that are mere forwards or unimportant messages.

4.   To avoid the more demanding tasks, we do the easier and smaller ones first, which are comparatively not as important as the challenging task at hand.

5.   Switch on the TV and start scrolling aimlessly through the channels.

6.   Some of us even stare out in the space for long, even that seems more interesting than work.

If any of the above circumstances appear familiar to you, you are unquestionably a part of the community called PROCRASTINATORS.

Presently to manage these issues, mental collaboration is critical. You need to set yourself up rationally that you will give your best to get over your procrastinating habits, which eventually deal with stressing at last moment uncompleted deadlines.

The most ideal approach to do is mental notes and Speaking out about your deadlines before loved ones. Through this, you would be able to make a jot down list right when you're beginning your day and at the end as well. For instance, if I need to do my laundry and pay some of my bills two days from now, I will plan my activities accordingly and make sure I don't hang out with friends or go to movies thinking I'll get done with my chores later. Continue reminding yourself that this task is significant, and its consequences would be unfavorable, such as an angry mom for delayed duties.

Bit by bit, it very well may be outlined as recognizing why you procrastinate. It can be because of a lower level of enthusiasm for the activity or intrinsic satisfaction derived through that work. Or feeling that the task is excessively complicated and ought to be left undone until later.

As you have comprehended what drives you to delay your work, get down on dealing with how to keep away from it. If the work is exhausting and unsatisfactory, at that point, consider making it fun through a few things. For example, play your preferred music while doing it, so you enjoy that time. Or compensate yourself once you complete the task. You can also think of the consequences of not getting the work done.

Tasks that appear to be a tough finish should be done by making parts of it. As these tasks are separated into less complicated, littler steps, it seems more straightforward to go about and complete it. The step by step procedure also holds a kind of feeling of accomplishment as you basically go through the ladder finishing every little piece of it. Organizing and planning your work and isolating significant with pressing tasks also improves the procedure and maintains a strategic distance from procrastination. The plan for the day should be to keep it going. What's more, continue empowering yourself mentally so that germs of procrastination don't sneak in!

Along these lines, quit overestimating the activities, and get down on doing them so that your pending tasks are wiped clean, and you can work on new projects, and start enjoying the fulfillment of finishing the job on time.

Procrastination drains confidence. For the most part, when one procrastinates, they would prefer not to confront or deal with something they dread. My mind thinks of expounding reasons to put off doing something in my procrastination experience, and I believe. Although, over the long haul, I begin to less capable and powerless. My feelings of dread become more generous, and I become increasingly frightened of taking a step of action. By one way or another, what I initially intended to do becomes considerably more terrifying than it did when I first set out to do it. Procrastination never leaves; however, you can adjust how you manage it. Everybody is unique, and relying upon your circumstance, some of you may delay for seven days, a month, or a year. Regardless of your pattern, when you utilize a useful tool to escape procrastination, the time you spend procrastinating diminishes. You figure out how to get yourself to act faster.

I have seen as a great instrument for conquering procrastination to immediately take a step of action. The quicker I act around the regions I need to fear, the easier it is to accomplish more. I additionally make requests of my customers to complete something before our next call. That way, it doesn't give them an excessive amount of time to consider it. You may think well imagine a scenario where I need to accomplish something that takes much more than one action step. For instance, you probably need to return to school. Start with one step, such as looking up different schools and getting few applications. You probably need to go into business, examine existing similar companies, and converse with self-employed individuals. These actions will get you out of procrastination and make more opportunities for you to pursue your goals.

Most of what causes procrastination is your psyche and what it is said to you, which you are presumably unaware of. Except if you decide to concentrate at the forefront of your thoughts and figure out how to relinquish debilitating thoughts, you will be a slave to them, strolling around unconscious, not having control over your life.

You may have thought, well, that sounds more difficult than one might expect. It is effortless once you begin. This is what I do in my own life and educate others: when I need to accomplish something that I am frightened of, my mind begins to think impairing thoughts; I recognize the dread and that I have to take an immediate step. If not, I will end up being a casualty of an unsupportive idea pattern. Something else I do is if it requires proceeded actions, I get support from others by talking to someone and telling them what I expect to do and ask that to consider me responsible.

Here's an example from Fred's life; Fred used to feel fearful and resistant to following up with prospective clients. He had feared they would get angry with him for calling them, or he would sound unclear and fumble over his words. Fred would put off calling them for so long that it would get more challenging for him to pick up the phone because he would come up with so many scary scenarios of what could happen. Fred started calling them before meeting them, but he had time to convince him. He always said to himself before getting: "What is the worst thing that can happen? They may refuse, not answer or call me back." "I can solve it." After the call, Fred His confidence will increase, and he will be proud of himself. Now, Fred has little or no fear of recruiting potential customers because he uses these tools.Overcoming procrastination and building self-confidence is a mixed way of working that requires continuous effort and continuous bold steps. Both are the most effective and primary methods to see excellent results at your confidence level.

Moving beyond procrastination is tied in with being honest with yourself, recognize where you have been procrastinating. Recall that this is not okay with you since it leaves you feeling debilitated, and you need to build your self-confidence. Perceive that making a prompt move toward the things you fear is perhaps the most ideal approach to stop and prevent procrastination. Pick one zone where you have been procrastinating in your life and focus on making three action steps over the week. Tell one individual in your life about the three action steps you focused on taking. Request that they consider you accountable by following up and supporting you.

Chapter 11: Step By Step Instructions To Beat Procrastination And Achieve Your Goals

The line between procrastination and inspiration can be skinny. At the point when you feel propelled, you're loaded with motivation, prepared to handle your projects, and you dive in headfirst. Procrastination makes you feel paralyzed: you may end up doing everything and something besides the task you should do. As opposed to moving you towards your goals, delaying keeps you stuck in a similar spot.

How can you move from procrastination to inspiration? There are a couple of useful thoughts you can execute immediately. In the first place, ask yourself what kind of procrastination you're experiencing? The "busy" type, where you'll find some other sort of activity to do (chores, TV, reading, socializing) other than what needs to get done? Or then again, the "empty" kind, where you play around, gaze at the screen, and don't get anything done at all? It doesn't make a difference which kind you're inflicted with. There are consistent approaches to beat procrastination and move towards your goals:

1. Make quantifiable goals. This is crucial. Be sure your goal is specific and measurable. For example, "Get fit" isn't quantifiable. How would you know when you've accomplished that objective? Alternately, "Lose 10% body fat" is very specific and measurable. Be sure every one of your goals is quantifiable.

2. Chunk down your goals. The best way to accomplish your goals and beat procrastination is one small step at a time. Break your massive goal into smaller goals, which ought to likewise be quantifiable. "work for three hours" might be a small step to accomplishing a more significant objective; however, more effective action would be "Finish Project A." When this small objective is finished, completed, and

tucked away, you can compensate yourself for a break. You'll likewise feel great about having a task finished, which will further motivate you to work.

3. Tell somebody about your goals. In case you're extremely genuine about kicking your procrastination habit, perhaps the best thing you can do is share your goals with another person. You need this individual to be somebody who will support you in accomplishing your goals, somebody who will be on your back and say, "Have you done it yet?" Sometimes getting things done for others, or having the help of others behind you, will give you the inspiration you have to quit procrastinating.

4. Get rational with yourself. It very well may be simple - and tempting - to put off doing things because your big goal appears to be so far away. Imagine yourself later on having accomplished your goal. Think about all the little steps you took to get there. Is there something you ought to do at this moment? Inspire yourself and continue working. Remember that what you do today will pay off. What you put off today doesn't mysteriously get done tomorrow. Big goals require lots of child accomplishments along the way. And these are all doable.

Make sure to keep that firm goal in your mind. Consider what one small step you need to take right now towards accomplishing your goal. Remember to get individuals to help you achieve your goal, and you'll be on track to completing self-discipline and beating procrastination.

Chapter 12: Ways To Stop Procrastinating And Get Things Done Accordingly

Procrastinating is a habit that a significant number of us frequently show in our lives. Rather than utilizing our opportunity to complete substantial tasks, we procrastinate to use our time on other unimportant things. When it is late, we hurry and panic to finish the job, resulting in inefficiency and failure (sometimes). Time is valuable, indeed. Therefore, we have to know and execute approaches to stop procrastinating and use our time.

Divide Your Task into Little Steps

A factor that causes us to procrastinate is that we feel overpowered by the job's gravity needing to be done. When we think it is too big for us to achieve, we will, in general, lose interest in it and disregard it. If we can break the entire task into smaller steps, it gets simpler to manage. Whenever broken into smaller parts, we start to think about the smaller job as quite simple; therefore, we are moved to make a prompt move.

Alter Your Working Environment

The environment we are working in can directly affect our productivity. For this, you may need to check out your working space and condition and decide if they move you to work or cause you to feel lazy. Decide whether your environment causes you to feel like you need only to rest and put off your tasks. If this is true, consider approaches to change the setting and make it progressively helpful for working. Replace your light bulbs with a brighter one; spray some aroma-therapeutic air spray that will awaken your sense, etc.

Make a Timeline/Deadline

With only one deadline, you additionally will, in general, procrastinate. This is because we happen to feel that we still have a long time to deal with it. When you have already divided the task into smaller parts, set a deadline for each of these smaller tasks. This way, you will start to think and feel that you should use your time more wisely. It creates an urgent feeling in you that will push you to act.

Eliminate What Makes You Procrastinate

There could be some pit stops or causes that lead you to procrastination. For example, check your browser to see which bookmarks can take more of your time yet are not very important. Segregate these bookmarks and place them in another folder that you cannot readily access. In other words, get rid of things that will distract you from your work. Turn off a radio or television that may sidetrack you from studying or finishing your work.

Be With People of Inspiration

If you need to feel increasingly idealistic throughout everyday life, probably the best advice you can get to stay in the company of hopeful individuals. The same rule is true with eliminating procrastination. Be with individuals who can inspire you to act, rather than individuals who will be more than ready to go along with you in your procrastination. Get a companion who can help make performing a task more fun. Together, you will be responsible for each other's plans and goals.

STOP PROCRASTINATION TIPS - DON'T MAKE ANY MORE EXCUSES NOW

We all hesitate to a small extent. However, if that habit becomes chronic, at that point, it can begin making issues throughout our life.

There are many terrible impacts of procrastination. So we have to find a way to bring this habit to an end.

The individual put forward many explanations behind the delay. First of all, these reasons may seem real. However, when you study it carefully, for these reasons, you will find loopholes. Here are some tips to help you avoid procrastination.

Stop Procrastination Tips

1. Do more than you think - there is a phenomenon called 'death by analysis.' This happens when individuals feel a lot about something, yet don't act. They plan widely; however, they fail to put the arrangement enthusiastically.

2. This happens because thinking is easy while doing it is challenging. We avoid accomplishing something as it requires effort, focus, and getting ourselves through brief trouble. So, as to quit procrastinating, think less, and accomplish more.

3. Start with the hardest task - First, do the most difficult task, so the rest of the things become simple. You can feel a great deal of weight lifting off from yourself.

4. You can discover less obstruction in finishing the rest of the task. They will feel pleasant to you because the most difficult, uncomfortable task is currently behind you.

5. Figure out how to deal with complex tasks - The main motivation behind why individuals procrastinate is that they feel a given task is a lot for them to deal with. They feel it is past their abilities, or it is excessively difficult!

6. A great method to conquer this is to separate the complex task into smaller and smaller pieces to trouble you any longer. Assume you need to go on a long journey. Break it into smaller steps with the goal that it doesn't look so big anymore.

a. Record the task you completed - When the day is finished, list all the activities you finished today. This will be useful in looking into how your day went and how profitable you have been.

If you do this consistently, you can find that your rundown of finished tasks is becoming ordinary. That means you are becoming increasingly beneficial as the day advances. Time to celebrate!

Remember that the above tips to stop procrastination will take time to master. Initially, you might face internal resistance but should fight it. Keep going till you can conquer or at least reduce this habit. Are you ready for the change?

HOW TO STOP PROCRASTINATION PROBLEM?

Most of the individuals are confronted with the question of how to stop procrastination and start achieving tasks? The choice of stopping procrastination rests with the people. When the choice is taken, the drafting of a plan for achieving success is significant. To maintain the plan is also essential for stopping procrastination.

Some practical steps are required to be followed while killing the problems of procrastination from its underlying foundations. When the answer to how to stop procrastination is found, the individuals' entire life pattern will change permanently. The appropriate response improves the people's genuine capability and encourages new inspiration, commitment, and vitality in taking care of the issues looked in life expectancy.

Reasons for procrastination:

There are various explanations for the procrastination habits of individuals. These reasons extend from the fear of success or failure or just plain laziness.

By recognizing the reasons for procrastination, a legitimate arrangement can be created for its destruction. This plan needs to revolve around how to stop procrastination. The plan will help the people in getting inspired in this manner, giving them a better life.

Self-confidence is the main consideration for inspiration. Fear of rejections, fear of failures, and the feeling of being undeserving or unworthy are the common reasons for procrastination. Making positive steps in building the self-confidence enhances the chances of getting motivated. The demonstration of procrastination in itself is a purpose behind the absence of self-confidence among the people. This gives rise to feelings of stress, tension, and blame, which prompts unfulfilled dreams and goals. This increases the need to find strategies on the most proficient method to stop procrastination.

Evaluation of Stopping Procrastination:

Pain and joy are the two important things that motivate individuals specifically. List the pleasures that might be normal by achieving the set goals is essential. Moreover, the posting of the disadvantages of procrastination for the set goals has additionally to be finished. Some measure of soul searching and assessment of the individual lives is quite fundamental. Defeating unreasonable frights, phobias, not keeping rewards in mind, and remaining focused encourages discovering how to stop procrastination. These are basic strides in raising the self-confidence of the people.

If people hate themselves because of the absence of courage to pursue their goals, they are setting themselves for disappointment throughout everyday life. The ending of old habits and supporting self-confidence are the fundamental activities that can welcome individuals to progress.

Procrastination is challenging to break and sets aside effort for its eradication. But, if the specific reasons for it are comprehended, it gets simpler for discovering how to stop procrastination.

Chapter 13: How To Stop Procrastination And Succeed

Procrastination In Your Occupation

Are you someone who is in every case late to work or appointments because your motivation is missing? Do you lose hours at work doing insignificant jobs and avoid getting going with the tasks you realize you ought to do. A vicious cycle can start for you. The more your delay is beginning that new project or priority task, the more pressure you can feel under, and the more likely you are to avoid it and procrastinate. A few people even change employers and occupations to abstain from the beginning or complete a task that they have prevaricated over.

You might be exhausted in your present place of employment, yet its security keeps you from leaving, and you feel trapped. The fear of what a new position may include prevents you from going after a new job that could re-inspire you. All the time you delay, your self-confidence is being dissolved, and your capacity to procrastinate grows.

Personal Life Procrastination

Have you remained in your relationship since it gives familiarity and a feeling of well-being? Is it better the devil you know, or would you say you fear being distant from everyone else? Has your relationship lost its sparkle? This can occur in any relationship, and it doesn't imply that you need to end it. The best relationship for you might be the one that you are in as of now. Except if you are available in the relationship and welcome it, you may feel miserable, lost, or simply trapped. Procrastination can become a feature of an individual relationship as well

Domestic Procrastination

Are the numbers of domestic jobs at home building up? Does your home need some fix or upkeep, for example, a cabinet that needs fixing or a broken pipe that should be solved? Sometimes, bringing in a tradesman to resolve a domestic issue can prompt procrastination. Instead of it being a simple job, no fixing it in time makes it a more expensive repair. You may have outstanding bills that you have not settled or other legal or challenging matters that need your attention, yet you still can't seem to handle.

Your home ought to be where you can loosen up and unwind, yet you may find that your house is never again that safe and secure haven. The un-started or incomplete jobs around your home simply add to a feeling of drift as the years pass by, and nothing changes.

Procrastination can harm many aspects of our lives. However, you don't need to keep enduring a life of malaise. If you envy others' achievement, it implies you perceive things can extraordinary and change. Yet procrastination is regularly only a perspective that anybody can fall casualty as well and recover from.

Perhaps you have attempted and (evidently) neglected to change previously. Possibly you have persuaded yourself that whatever you don't do anything will improve for you. There is a typical cynical saying that you might be comfortable with: "I ought to acknowledge my lot." If you have utilized it yourself, at that point, stop it now. It doesn't serve you in any capacity other than to keep you trapped as you seem to be.

Stop Your Procrastination

Understanding procrastination can likewise give insights to getting away from it as well. At first, approach things slowly and carefully. Try not to squeeze yourself by focusing on an excessive number of goals.

This methodology can overpower you. Keep it easy to begin with, and focus on tasks, goals, accomplishments that are simple for you. Little and simple goals are bound to be accomplished. In getting your feeling of progress, regardless of how small, you are bound to then have the option to achieve more significant and longer-term goals.

Start today to see yourself differently and stop using any negative self-labels. If you see yourself succeeding and carrying out those tasks and jobs, you are much more prone to succeed ((research has shown this). If you label yourself with names, for example, useless, lazy, or other unhelpful descriptive words, it will undermine your capacity to motivate yourself and make those exceptionally significant changes.

If you change how you envision yourself and drop the negative names, you will think it's simpler to gain ground.

One of the communist life challenges Steven Harold, subliminal specialists' helps individuals with is goal accomplishment and ending procrastination. Whether you are employed or independently employed, are musicians, entertainers, sports individuals, or have goals at home or in a relationship. Steven has helped individuals in every one of these areas and many others.

He has helped individuals discover new life in their current relationship in the domestic area just as finding a workable pace domestic task.

Sometimes an individual has had a past encounter that has prompted lost inspiration and procrastination. In hypnotherapy, it very well may be successful in returning to an event and change how you perceive it today.

Procrastination isn't something you acquired, yet you may have been affected by others. Procrastination is a habit, yet it doesn't need to be a lifestyle and living. As individuals, we are genuinely versatile and change habits frequently. Hypnotherapy can support your choice to quit procrastinating and, rather than feeling a victim of it, assume responsibility for your life.

Chapter 14: Time Management: 10 Strategies To Maximize Productivity And Minimize Stress

Do you stroll into work toward the beginning of the day, confident, quiet, and energized for another stimulating day? Or then again, do you fear to step into the workplace knowing when you sit down the telephone will ring, interferences start, fires spring up and should be put out, and regardless of what direction you turn, a person or thing is by all accounts requesting your attention?

If you ever experience long periods of overpowering, interruptions, interferences, and utter feelings of inadequacy - don't stress - you aren't the only one. In the present business condition, individuals are being approached to achieve increasingly more in less time with less help. This book presents 10 practical time management tips that will help you take back control of your workday and increase the likelihood you will leave the office with a feeling of accomplishment and success after a fulfilling day's work.

Plan each day. Planning your day puts you in charge of what is probably going to transpire. Start by using an electronic or online schedule and start to plan your workdays ahead of time. If your day requires that you keep time block open for unexpected events, plan unassigned time for those events. The additional time you dedicate to planning your days ahead of time and booking what you will take a shot when and the more determined you are to stick to the timetable will probably start to encounter super-gainful days. Proactive timetable administration expands your chances of success immensely. As the platitude goes, "By neglecting to design, you are planning to come up short."

1. **Simplify and Prioritize.**

Time-consuming and insignificant tasks (like perusing and noting each email you get) can consume a great deal of extra time for the day. Organize your task arranged by significance based on your responsibilities. Characterize basic day by day responsibilities and exercises you should perform to guarantee individual and business achievement. Schedule those things first, and don't proceed onward to different tasks until your most basic things are finished. When you have completed the basic tasks, consider some support time toward the workday's finish to answer messages, total desk work, and work on ventures that aren't straightforwardly identified with your most basic tasks.

2. **Just say no.**

Before you agree to assist a colleague or take on another task, consider the task you recognized in step number 2. If you don't have the vital time accessible or the project isn't exactly fit your range of abilities or responsibilities - simply state no. Taking on a project you don't possess energy for and will perform ineffectively on, the best-case scenario will just occupy you from what it is you are best at. Thus you will wind up being unremarkable in all areas, and your odds of accomplishment will decrease dramatically. Simplifying and choosing to state no is hard for most of us - yet is essential to keeping up balance and making differing degrees of progress.

3. **Delegate**.

Review your responsibilities and plan your day's work, and delegate unnecessary activities to other colleagues who are more qualified to handle the task.

The more carefully you focus on what you do best, the sooner you start to get results. If you have no other colleagues, you can delegate, look for ways to redistribute unnecessary activities to other companies.

There are many smart and effective ways to remove daily tasks from daily tasks by finding more suitable and willing people to take care of these items. As efficiency and achievement increase in different areas, you will find that the guesswork about additional compensation or fees you make will return to both of you for a long or long time.

4. Slow down and do it right the first time.

Rushing through projects and finishing them without being careful and permitting sufficient time for the survey is just setting yourself up for disappointment and future issues. Easing back down may add some extra time to the projects; however, setting aside the effort to guarantee everything is finished precisely will reduce problems further down the road. You will often find yourself spending a few times longer fixing an issue or curing a circumstance in the wake of something that has turned out badly. Slow down and take into consideration plentiful time to finish all errands precisely and totally.

5. Break large projects down into smaller individual tasks.

If you like large and complex events and break them down into individual tasks, it is much easier to give yourself honor and feel that you will continue to improve. When you complete each task, although you may not have completed the task, you will feel that you have achieved it, and you are more likely to praise yourself for it. Each achievement reaffirms that you are sincerely trying and working hard to achieve your goals—the ultimate goal.

6. Allow yourself to limit time spent on "dreaded" projects.

If you end up being assigned a project that you worry about, don't delay. The common behavior is usually to put the project in the background-until; the deadline is finally displayed, and you never decide.

Instead of sticking to the end and being forced to fight through the entire task-divide it into pieces and handle the small pieces reliably. Plan to shoot the project every day. You may find that starting from a part, you can achieve more than you initially expected. By doing this proactively over a couple of days, you will discover as the deadline time approaches you have the basic assignments finished and are prepared to proceed onward to an increasingly agreeable project.

7. **Take a look in the mirror.**

Monitor what you do and where you invest your energy throughout the week. Be straightforward with yourself, take a gander at each connection consistently and decide whether you are utilizing your time profitably and successfully. In a week, harmless habits add up to a giant productivity killer, and you are usually surprised. Focus on changing any non-supportive habits you encounter.

8. **Limit distractions.**

Set aside time to focus on broad or basic projects. In the meantime, please close the office door, close the phone, close the email, and ask your colleague to help you take a vacation with a trivial interruption.

9. **Exercise, eat healthily, and make sure you get the sleep your body needs.**

Exercise, rest, and proper nourishment guarantees you have the energy required to be playful and gainful all through the whole workday. By keeping up adequate health and balance in life, you will get yourself ready to achieve more, which leads to increased success and more time away from work. Working less saves extra time to concentrate on parity and health, and the cycle begins to build momentum. Work less, get progressively cultivated in less time, and experience a more beneficial healthy lifestyle.

These 10 time management and productivity tips, when taken individually, can prove to be very useful in increasing your productivity and effectiveness. When combined as a group, I guarantee your workday will transform itself within 60 days or less. Start slowly and implement one or two items per week until you feel comfortable with maintaining new habits. As you build momentum and gain confidence, you will find yourself able to simultaneously implement these strategies, and your results will skyrocket.

Chapter 15: 3 Ways To Maximize Productivity In Your Business

How might anybody balance business and family obligations and responsibilities and still have time left over for some personal enjoyment and relaxation?

The appropriate responses are SIMPLE; however, I should caution you they aren't, in every case, EASY. Here are 3 hints for improving your productivity now.

Stay in the present as much as possible.

STOP multi-tasking. There, I said it. Regardless of whether you are male or female, I, for one, don't trust it is humanly possible to multi-task and achieve as much as though you focused on a single task and center around accomplishing the most ideal outcome in the base measure of time required.

This requires you to design your days and task ahead of time and limit interruptions and disturbances. Concentrate on the 3 basic tasks you can achieve today, and don't let some other interruptions remove time from these tasks until you complete them. If your layout these critical daily tasks required of you and minimize all other distractions until you are complete, you are well on your way to producing maximum results.

Schedule your days in advance.

To keep up top efficiency, your workdays must stay organized and predictable to deliver the most extreme outcomes. Preceding going home every day, invest time prioritizing the assignments tomorrow, and the order they will be finished. Furthermore, before leaving the workplace on Friday evening, spend time laying out the basic framework of each day the next week.

Hope schedule as many of your meetings and duties as out of sight could be expected under the circumstances and possibly work new things if they overshadow existing arrangements or fit into zones you at present don't have anything booked.

Working your schedule along these lines makes it simple to state NO when new things spring up. You can virtually depend on your current schedule and decrease when you have an arrangement booked. Regardless of whether the arrangement is going for an hour to stroll in the recreation center, you are being straightforward with the individual mentioning your time...you are reserved, and they should choose from the following accessible open arrangement.

Delegate and follow-up consistently.

Most of us have already undertaken some form of delegation. Unfortunately, inconsistent and ineffective delegation often will only compound the challenge faced when maximizing your productivity. Simply delegating tasks is not enough to improve productivity since you will often spend as much or more time repairing the damage ineffective delegation can cause. Effective delegation involves communicating the delegation's goals and objectives and, most importantly, requires consistent follow-up after the delegation. Too many people delegate without follow-up and then end up extremely frustrated when spending countless hours redoing work that didn't end up as intended. To ensure you receive the type of work you expect, it is critical you follow-up immediately after delegation to ensure the concepts were understood. Do this multiple times during the process to ensure results are on track, and most importantly, during the final stages of project completion to confirm the actual outcome reflects your desired results.

By implementing these SIMPLE techniques, you will begin to experience consistent gains in personal and professional productivity. Constant focus and practice over the upcoming months will ensure you commit the practice to habit and experience positive results in the years to follow.

Chapter 16: Why Do You Need To Be Persistent?

Let's first investigate the meaning of the word persistence.

Persistence: firm or obstinate continuance in a strategy disregarding trouble or resistance. Persistence is a characteristic that is an "absolute necessity" if you need to accomplish your goals throughout everyday life. Without the capacity to continue through hardships, you're odds of accomplishing, your goals are thin. Luckily, Persistence can be created, and it can turn into a lifestyle once you start to rehearse and comprehend its significance to the accomplishment of your goals.

The most effective method to Be Persistent

The undeniable answer is to continue progressing in the direction of your goal until you accomplish it; however, what does it truly take to keep your eye on the prize in any event when all the signs are advising you to surrender? Be irrational and be preposterous about the accomplishment of your goals. You have to get settled with being crazy, absurd, ridiculous, and determined. Those are a few terms that individuals will begin to throw at you when they see you seeking after your goals, although it might appear to be unthinkable. It is alright to act in a specific way to get what you need; nonetheless, that doesn't characterize who you're except if you need it to.

If you need to act insane and amazingly extroverted to achieve your goals, at that point, do it; however, once you accomplish your goals, you can choose whether you need to return to the old you or on if you need to keep on being insane and extroverted.

Determination isn't about pursuing your goal when it seems right; it's about following your goals even when you're getting little to no results, and you feel like you're wasting your time.

You must choose between limited options. Except if you've been given a silver-spoon and you were brought up in a family with heaps of riches and connections, you should be happy to continue to accomplish your goals. The moment you choose to surrender, your fantasies, goals, and desires will become history. If you need to accomplish your goals throughout everyday life, you need to continue; in such a case that you don't, you Will Not accomplish your goals.

Persistence needs to become inevitable the minute you commit to a goal. If there was one success characteristic that you should have to be effective, it would be persistence. It doesn't make a difference if it takes two or three weeks to accomplish your goal or a few years. Regardless of the extent to which it takes, it will all be justified when you achieve your goal, despite all the trouble.

Chapter 17: Persistence And Will-Power

Persistence is the capacity to proceed through misfortune, to get over the disappointment and 'go-ahead' for our goals. Abraham Lincoln, an early leader of the United States, alluded to diligence as "the Ability to Maintain Action Regardless of your emotions. Push on even when you want to stop". Persistence is a perspective. When an individual seeks after any big goal, their inspiration will vary, starting with one day then onto the next. Now and again, they will feel motivated, once in a while, not. But it's not inspiration that produces results — it's actions.

1 'Comfort Zone' is the state of your life to which you are accustomed and which most are

Reluctant to change, constancy permits an individual to act in any event when they don't feel motivated to do as such. If an individual essentially pushes on making a move, notwithstanding troubles, disappointment, or protection from continue working, they will eventually get results, and results will ultimately give its inspiration. For instance, a woman endeavoring to get more fit turns into much increasingly eager about dieting and exercising once she lost those first 10 pounds and felt her clothes fitting more loosely. Two traditional perseverance are Thomas Edison and Abraham Lincoln Edison succeeded in inventing the first electric bulb after spending \$40,000 and performing 1200 experiments. Imagine a scenario in which he stopped in 1199. We would all be sitting in the dark! Life is always full of setbacks, and failures always precede successes.

Any practical individual needs to experience these deterrents and disappointments. Abraham, President of the United States, failed repeatedly before winning an election and got to be one of the best U.S Presidents.

Edison has said that "since something doesn't do what you arranged it to do doesn't mean it's useless... Switches should be a motivation for extraordinary achievement. Why, man, I have gotten loads of results! If I find 10,000 different ways, something won't work. I am not discouraged because every wrong attempt discarded is just one more step forward... There are no guidelines; we're simply attempting to achieve something." Obstacles and disappointments are adverse, yet they can be learning encounters or openings that push an individual to invest more energy. The overcoming of obstacles can strengthen a person and offer progressive measurement of their growing strength. Discouragement creeps in when encountering difficult obstacles, and repeated failure can cause a person to question their goals and faith in themselves. This leads to self-doubt and the loss of self-confidence. In this situation, a person has to refocus on their ideas and dreams. Persistence is a process of re-decision making. One can train himself/herself to be a persistent person. Napoleon Hill gives eight factors that persistence is based upon:

Definite reason – realize what you need.

- Desire

- Self-dependence - the belief to do your plan

- Definite plans - written organized plan.

- Accurate information - realizing your plan is sound.

- Cooperation - being with other people who will assist you in creating persistence.

- Will control - focus your thoughts on acquiring your objectives.

- Habit - persistence is a propensity that can be intentionally developed.

The most effective method to Develop Persistence:

1. Have a positive reason backed up with a powerful urge to acquire it. Record it.

2. Have a game plan. How are you going to get it going? What do you have to do?

3. Close your mind to negativity and discouraging influences. Self-talk can be the most harmful.

4. Watch which were saying to yourself.

Build up a group of individuals who will support you and consider you responsible for finishing your actions. When to give up, should you generally persevere and never surrender? Surely not. In some cases, submitting is the best alternative. Have you at any point known about an organization called Traf-O-Data? Shouldn't something is said about Microsoft? Bill Gates and Paul Allen started the two organizations.

Traf-O-Data was the first organization they began in 1972. Gates and Allen ran it for quite a while before quitting. They surrendered. They improved Microsoft. If they hadn't abandoned Traf-O-Data, at that point, they probably wouldn't have made their progress with Microsoft. So how would you realize when to press on or when to surrender? Probably the most ideal way is to ask yourself these questions: Is your plan still correct? If not, update the plan. Is your goal, right? If not, update or desert your goal. There's no respect in sticking to a goal that never again moves you. Diligence isn't determination.

Persistence for Goals

Goals are tangible achievements that drive one's inspiration and structure one's meanings of accomplishments and victories.

Eleanor Roosevelt advises us that "the future has a place with the individuals who trust in the excellence they had always wanted." Defining objectives is frequently talked about as dreaming a fantasy. Objective interest is wandering out, traveling over a foggy ocean towards an island. It requires a lot of confidence.

Goal Setting Technique

- Put a goal on paper in as extraordinary detail as possible will allow you to see the individual advances you have to take.

- Take the more significant arrangement and chunk it down into smaller interim goals.

- Work on arriving at your objective by tackling a smaller goal each day or each week. This makes your guide to your individual goal with all the focal points along the way.

Attributes of Goals

All objectives, regardless of whether short-term or long-term, should consolidate these basic traits:

a. Be sensible. Goals should be based on your abilities and circumstances.

b. Be possible. Try not to set up limitations that make the sensible ridiculous.

c. Be adaptable. Anticipate hindrances and hope to work around them.

d. Be quantifiable. Have an objective at the top of the priority list so you know when you have arrived at your objective.

e. Be heavily influenced by you. Set your objectives dependent on your qualities, interests, and wants. Target things where you can control the result.

Winston Churchill gave a discourse precisely 60 years prior on October 29, 1946. These words are as yet appropriate today. "Never yield - never, never, never, never, in nothing extraordinary or little, huge or unimportant, never give in but to feelings of respect and great sense. Never respected power; never respected the overpowering may of the foe." The 'Emblem of our college may empower you to comprehend this better. Our life resembles "A Ship in the Sea." This symbolizes we need to continue battling and confronting various troubles in the ocean of life, much the same as a boat or a vessel that overcomes substantial storms, winds, and sun. This ought to consistently advise us that "Life is a Struggle" or "To Live is to Struggle" against the issues and challenges and not surrender. Remain centered. Never change your objective – simply your methodology. Perseverance must turn into a lifestyle if you need to succeed. By figuring out how to conquer issues and snags, you can turn into an excellent individual. There is a tune sung by Mariah Carey. Some portion of the melody says that—"There can be marvels, When you accept, Though trust is slight It's difficult to execute Who recognizes what wonders You can accomplish When you trust Somehow you will, … You will when you accept." However, troublesome life is being firm in your fantasies and objectives and having confidence in yourself. Endeavor on. What appears to be difficult to accomplish will be accomplished.

Hard Work

Difficult work is the last segment, yet it isn't the least supposing that an individual isn't focused on working hard for a goal, he/ she cannot be successful. This is predictable to AU Motto "Work OMNIA VINCIT".

This Latin witticism signifies, "Productive exertion vanquishes all things". We can conquer all challenges through difficult work. We work not exclusively to procure cash professionally just, yet also for making an important life.

We accept that one regulates oneself and one's reality by the honorability of one's work, which incorporates enterprising exertion, responsibility, assurance, and mental fortitude to confront affliction.

Your capacity to accomplish your happiness is the genuine proportion of your achievement throughout everyday life. Nothing is increasingly significant. Nothing can supplant it. If you achieve everything of a material sort, yet you are upset, you have failed at satisfying your potential as an individual.

You can genuinely be upbeat when you practice self-control, self-dominance, and restraint. When you feel that you are in finished control of your life, you are content.

Chapter 18: Discipline And Happiness

You feel unhappy with the degree to which you feel you are not in control or constrained by different factors or individuals." Psychologists consider this your "locus of control." There are fifty years of research and several books and articles regarding this matter. They all presume that pressure and misery emerge when you feel constrained by outside conditions. This is clarified as the contrast between an "inside locus of control" (glad) and an "outer locus of control" (unhappy). You have an interior locus of control when you feel that you are in control; you settle on your own choices, and what occurs you in life is, to a great extent, controlled without anyone else. At the point when you have an inner locus of control, you feel that you are in the driver's seat of your own life and that you are in the driver's seat. You feel that you decide the greater part of what befalls you. Thus, you feel solid, deliberate, and glad. Then again, you have an external locus of control over how much you feel that you are not in charge or have little capacity to coordinate your own life. For instance, if you feel that a self-assertive or basic chief constrains you, however, you can't bear to lose your employment since you have no reserve funds set aside, you experience significant levels of pressure and tension. This makes you make a less than impressive display, which makes it significantly more probable that your troublesome manager will fire you, and this all the time realizes precisely the conditions you fear.

Another example is that you may feel you are constrained by an awful marriage or relationship from which you can't getaway. You may feel constrained by your bills, by the cash you owe, and your commitments to keep up your way of life. You may feel that you are denied by your state of being or absence of instruction.

Numerous individuals feel that their past constrains them in light of troublesome adolescence or childhood and that there is nothing they can do to change their circumstances. Numerous individuals feel that their characters constrain them and that they are not ready to improve. They state, "That is only how I am." By saying this, they forgive themselves of all obligation regarding applying the essential control and self-control to roll out the improvements they realize they have to make to carry on with the sort of life they need to live and be glad. The way to supplanting an external locus of control with an inward locus of control is for you to conclude today to take total charge of your life. Acknowledge and acknowledge that you settle on your own choices and that you are the place you are and what you are a direct result of yourself. If there is some zone in your life where you are distraught, teach yourself to take the necessary steps to change the circumstance.

The Reason for Happiness

It is regularly the hole's size between your current circumstance and the conditions and circumstances that you feel that you should be glad that decides if you are cheerful or miserable. This is mainly your very own matter of assessment and choice. A familiar adage is that "achievement is getting what you need; satisfaction is wanting what you get." When your pay and life are steady with your objectives and desires, and you are content with your circumstance, you feel cheerful. If then again, under any circumstances, your present circumstance is not quite the same as what you truly need and expect, you will be malcontented and miserable. This condition of satisfaction can be continually evolving. At the point when you start your vocation, a salary of $50,000 every year can appear to be an enormous accomplishment. In any case, when you arrive at this objective, you start to be unhappy because you are not earning $100,000 or more. Some people are unhappy earning a million dollars a year.

Happiness Is a By-Product

The intriguing thing about happiness is that it's anything but a goal that you can focus on and accomplish all by yourself; satisfaction is a result that comes to you when you are occupied with accomplishing something that you genuinely appreciate while in the company of individuals who you like and regard. Lord Nightingale, maybe the most acclaimed and regarded radio reporter on accomplishment ever, said that "satisfaction is the dynamic acknowledgment of a commendable perfect." Whenever you feel that you are moving, bit by bit, toward something essential to you, toward your most significant objectives, you naturally feel happy. You feel fulfilled and content. You feel a colossal feeling of self-improvement and prosperity.

Five Ingredients of Happiness Self-discipline is essential to happiness. Self-control requires both to decide what happiness intends for you and that you work continuously every day toward accomplishing that perfect condition. As far as I can tell and lessons, I have discovered five fixings to joy. A setback in any of these territories can cause pressure, misery, and a crazy sentiment.

Five Ingredients of Happiness

1. Health and energy. This is maybe the most significant component of a decent life. We make progress toward it for our entire lives. It is just when you appreciate significant levels of pain-free health and a constant flow of vitality that you feel genuinely cheerful.

As a rule, health is a "deficiency need." This implies you don't consider your health, especially until you are denied it. For instance, you don't consider your teeth until you have a toothache. You don't consider your body until you have throbs or agonies of some kind.

You must use discipline and willpower throughout your life to achieve high levels of health and fitness.

2. Happy relationships. Ultimately 85 percent of your happiness—or unhappiness—will come from your relationships with other people. As Aristotle stated, "Man is a social creature." We are intended to work in the public arena, working and living with others at each phase of our lives. Your capacity to go into and keep up great associations with your mate, youngsters, companions, partners, and others is the genuine proportion of your character's nature and your degree of emotional wellness. Individuals with high confidence and dignity coexist better with others and have a lot more joyful lives. Perhaps the most significant misstep is to underestimate our connections, particularly our most significant ones. We frequently don't consider them until there is an issue, and afterward, we assume nothing else.

3. Meaningful work. To be truly happy, you should be completely engaged in life. You should do things that keep you active and give you a feeling of satisfaction. If you are making a living, you should accomplish work that you appreciate, progress admirably, and for which you are generously compensated. Individuals are cheerful just when they believe they are committing some kind, they are placing in more than they are taking out.

You have to feel that what you do truly has any effect on others' lives and work. In investigations of representative inspiration, bosses imagine that individuals are fundamentally motivated by cash and advantages. In any case, when representatives are overviewed, the three factors that persuade them the most end up being testing and intriguing work; open doors for development and progression; and charming collaborators.

One of your most significant duties to yourself is to secure the correct position for you, and afterward, when you have it, toss your entire heart into it. On the off chance that you don't want to place your entire heart into your work in any way, shape, or form, it might be inadequate regarding at least one of the three basics to a positive work environment. It might be an indication this isn't the right place for you.

4. Financial independence. Probably the most significant feelings of fear we experience are those of misfortune, disappointment, and poverty. We fear being down and out, without assets, and reliant on others. One of your main obligations to yourself is to progress in the direction of financial independence and money related opportunity for a mind-blowing duration. Surprisingly, most joyful individuals have arrived at where they never again stress over cash. This isn't something you can leave to risk, yet rather something that requires conscious, intentional activity and enormous self-discipline to accomplish. At whatever point you feel that there is a major hole between where you are today financially and where you might in a perfect world want to be, you experience pressure, stress, and misery.

5. Self-completion. This is the inclination that you are turning out to be all you are equipped for turning out to be. This happens when you feel that you are acknowledging increasingly more of your actual potential. Abraham Maslow is most popular for his Hierarchy of Needs. He confirmed that individuals have both "inadequacy needs" and "being needs." People endeavor either to make up for their insufficiencies or to understand their possibilities. He reasoned that you start to advance and create the most elevated levels workable for you just when your lack needs are first fulfilled.

Deficiency Needs.

Your first deficiency need is for security and endurance. Fulfilling this need requires that you have adequate food, water, clothing, and convenience to preserve your life and well-being. If your safety or survival is threatened in any way, you will turn out to be completely engrossed in satisfying this need. You will encounter huge pressure, and you will be totally troubled until you are safe again. For instance, consider being in a dangerous circumstance.

The second deficiency needs that Maslow recognized is the requirement for security. This need grasps money related, enthusiastic, and physical security. You have to have enough cash to accommodate yourself, security in your relationship at work and at home, and physical security to guarantee that you are not at risk of any sort. If your security needs are compromised, you become distracted by them. For instance, consider losing your activity unexpectedly: How might you feel?

The third deficiency needs that Maslow identified is belongingness. Every individual needs to be in social relationships with others, both at home and at work. You should be perceived and acknowledged by others in your reality. Every individual should be agreeable in their associations with others and seen and acknowledged as part of a team or group.

Self Esteem Needs.

When you have accomplished a sufficient level of every one of these fundamental needs—well-being, security, and belongingness—you at that point go to fulfill the higher requirements for self-esteem and self-worth, your being needs.

Your self-esteem is the center of your character and, to a great extent, decides how you feel about everything that transpires. All that you do in life is to build your self-esteem or shield it from being decreased. Your confidence—how you feel about yourself and the amount you like and worth yourself—determines your happiness more than another single factor. Your confidence originates from numerous components. At the point when you are enjoyed and acknowledged by others, living reliably with your most noteworthy qualities, working admirably and being perceived for it, and moving dynamically toward the accomplishment of your objectives and goals, at that point, you normally feel upbeat and fulfilled. You feel valued and very much in control.

The Highest Human Need.

The most significant need that Maslow distinguished was for self-completion. He reasoned that less than 2 percent of the population ever arrives at this stature of individual satisfaction. A great many people remain so engrossed with their insufficiency needs and securing or improving their confidence their ego needs that they give little thought or effort to self-actualization. In any case, it is just when you understand that you have enormous individual potential and start endeavoring to do, be, and have like never before in some territory that you start to encounter self-completion and genuine bliss.

The happiest of all people feel that they are accomplishing something beneficial and vital to their lives. They believe they are extending and moving past anything they've at any point done previously. Individuals gave to self-realization might be composing books or making masterpieces. They might be ascending mountains or contending in sports. They might be building organizations or scaling the statures of their callings.

The brilliant thing about self-realization needs is that they can never be fulfilled. As you constantly endeavor for a mind-blowing duration to be and have and accomplish like never before previously, you experience a consistent progression of bliss and happiness. You feel that you are getting increasingly more of what you were intended to turn into.

Chapter 19: The Discipline Of Persistence

The best self-control test is the point at which you persevere notwithstanding difficulty, and you drive yourself forward to finish your undertakings 100%, regardless of how you feel.

Courage has two parts: The first part is the courage to start, to begin, to dispatch forward without any assurances of achievement. The second part is the courage to endure, to persist when you feel discouraged and want to quit.

a. Your constancy is simply the measure of your belief in yourself and in what you are doing.

b. The more you have confidence in the integrity and rightness of what you are doing, the more you will continue.

c. The more you persevere, the more you will, in general, have faith in yourself and what you are doing. The standards are reversible!

d. Constancy is self-control in real life.

e. Self-discipline prompts confidence, a more prominent feeling of individual force, which prompts more prominent perseverance, which prompts significantly more prominent self-control in an upward winding.

f. "Persistence is to the character of man or lady as carbon is to steel." (Napoleon Hill)

g. You improve yourself into a stronger individual by persisting when you want to stop.

You take complete control over the development of your character. Eventually, you become unstoppable.

The benefits of practicing self-discipline in every area of your life are many:

1. The habit of self-discipline virtually guarantees your success in life, both with others and yourself.

2. You will get more done, faster, and of higher quality with discipline than with any other skill.

3. You will be paid more and promoted more quickly.

4. You will experience a greater sense of self-control, self-reliance, and personal power.

5. Self-discipline is the key to self-esteem, self-respect, and personal pride.

6. The greater your self-discipline, the greater your self-confidence, and the lower will be your fear of disappointment and dismissal. Nothing will stop you.

7. With self-discipline, you will have the strength of character to persist over all obstacles until you eventually succeed. Start today to rehearse self-control in each aspect of your life. Endure right now self-restraint comes to you as consequently and as effectively as taking in and breathing out. Your future will be ensured.

Contemplations are causes, and conditions are impacts. In this manner, the nature of your reasoning, to a great extent, decides an incredible nature. The best mental rule is that "you become your opinion of more often than not." Top individuals in each field are seriously arrangement situated. They consider arrangements more often than not, rather than getting impeded in who did or didn't accomplish who knows what, the best individuals in each field focus on the arrangements and what should be possible to take care of the issue.

The Sufi thinker Izrhat Khan once stated, "Life is a persistent progression of issues, similar to waves from the sea.

They never stop." This implies your capacity to rehearse self-restraint, self-mastery, and discretion when confronted with the ceaseless progression of issues, challenges, difficulties, and impermanent disappointments you will encounter is fundamental to your achievement in business and throughout everyday life. The Inevitable and Unavoidable Crisis Throughout your life, you will confront a stream of physical, budgetary, family, business, and political issues. The main break right now chain of issues will be the infrequent emergency. If you are carrying on with a typical life, you will presumably encounter an emergency each a few months. Also, in these emergencies, you genuinely exhibit your character's nature and your character's quality. It is just when you face unforeseen inversions and misfortunes that you show the world what you are made of. All of life is a "test." The main inquiry for you is do you pass or fall flat? By their very nature, emergencies come "unbidden." You have no admonition or capacity to envision them ahead of time. If you did, it wouldn't be an emergency in any case — clearly, or you would as of now be readied. At the point when the inescapable emergency happens, more than at some other time, self-restraint is required so you can keep quiet and composed to manage the crisis adequately.

Perform at Your Best When something turns out badly, the common propensity of a great many people is to lose control and search for somebody to a fault. In any case, this is a misuse of vitality. It illuminates nothing. Instead, you should train yourself to resist the urge to panic, objective, and dispassionate. When you face a startling issue or emergency, train yourself to remain quiet and concentrate on the arrangement instead of the issue.

Think as far as what should be possible now, instead of deduction about how it happened and who is to be faulted. Like a mishap where somebody is harmed, you center around thinking about the harmed individual, halting the dying, and limiting the harm before you begin dissecting what and how it occurred. Practice self-control when managing an issue or emergency by promptly saying, "I am mindful," regardless of whether, at that point, you are capable just of controlling your reactions.

Keep Your Mind Clear

Top individuals have built up the capacity to react viably to an emergency, to resist the urge to panic, loose, and clear-peered toward. They train themselves to remain cool and numb. This empowers them to think all the more, dissect the circumstance impartially, and settle on better choices. Yet, the minute you become furious and disturbed, your neocortex — or your "thinking cerebrum" — closes down. All you have left at that point is your paleocortex, your enthusiastic cerebrum, which thinks as far as "battle or flight." When your passionate mind is in control, you think as far as highly contrasting, yes or no, or accomplishing something or sitting idle. You lose the capacity to think in shades of dim and take a gander at all the various potential approaches to managing this specific circumstance. Top individuals understand that each issue is a chance to develop restraint and individual certainty. You will ascend in life to the stature of the issues you are equipped for settling.

Venturing Stones to Success

A few years prior, Dr. Lawrence Peter composed a book called The Peter Principle.

It was an entertaining book with a focal theory that slice excessively near and dear.

He composed that in each association, individuals keep on being advanced until they arrive at a level where they are never again able to take care of the issues at that level. This is the place they stop and remain for the remainder of their professions. Moreover, every association is inevitably staffed by individuals who have arrived at their degree of ineptitude. This is particularly valid in the government. It is the essential motivation behind why the government is so time-and cost-wasteful, making it hard to complete anything by any stretch of the imagination. This usually is valid in any huge organization. You keep on ascending in your organization and your calling to your capacity to take care of the issues and settle on your profession's vital choices. Fortunately, when you consider arrangements more often than not, you train your mind to be seriously arrangement situated. Regardless of what issues or troubles emerge around you, your cerebrum will be consistently looking for inventive approaches to tackle the issue. Subsequently, you become more intelligent and speedier, with a greater amount of your reasoning cerebrum accessible to you quicker. On the off chance that you need to gain proficiency with a physical game, you start by learning the essential moves, and afterward, the further developed moves. You practice these aptitudes again and again until you can perform them and make a halfhearted effort normally and effectively inevitably. To ace the control of critical thinking, you have to build up a recipe or strategy that empowers you to manage practically any issue you face throughout your vocation or individual life. Luckily, there is a demonstrated equation for critical thinking and dynamic that you can utilize in almost any circumstance.

Chapter 20: A Nine-Step Method For Solving Problems Effectively

Stage 1: Take the Time to Define the Problem Clearly. In medication, they state that "precise finding is a large portion of the fix." Therefore, you have to ask, "What precisely is the issue?" It is completely stunning how a few people can get annoyed about an issue in an association; however, they all have an alternate thought or meaning of the specific idea of the issue they're confronting. Your main responsibility is to accomplish lucidity and to get everybody to concede to the meaning of the issue before you proceed onward to the matter of unraveling it.

Stage 2: Ask,

"Is It a Problem?" Remember, there are a few things that you can fail to address. They're not issues; they are only unavoidable issues facing everyone. On the off chance that loan costs rise or the subprime contract showcase falls, this can't issue. It can't that is amiable to an answer. Instead, it is something that must be worked around and managed.

Additionally, what gives off an impression of being an issue or a misfortune is an open door in a mask. At times, the issue shouldn't be unraveled by any means. Instead, you are currently allowed to accomplish something unique — which may be far better for you and your association.

Stage 3: Ask,

"What Else Is the Problem?" Beware of any issue for which there is just a single definition. The more ways you can characterize an issue, the almost certain it is to locate the best arrangement.

When we work with companies in which deals are beneath an ideal level, we compel them to ask twenty-one inquiries, all of which are various methods for repeating the issue. Whenever acknowledged as the right definition, every rehashing of the issue prompts an alternate arrangement and frequently a unique course for the association. For instance, we will ask, "What is the issue?" The principal answer is, "Our deals are excessively low." The following inquiry is, "The thing that else is the issue?" Answer: "Our rival's deals are excessively high." Notice the distinction. If the issue is that your deals are excessively low, the arrangement might be to expand your publicizing and advancement and hamburger up your business exercises. Suppose the definition is that your rival's deals are excessively high. In that case, the appropriate response might be to improve your items, change your product offering, bring down your costs, or go into a unique business by and large. By posing and noting a progression of inquiries like this, we, in the end, locate the right definition, one that is agreeable to a serviceable arrangement.

Stage 4: Ask,

"How Did This Problem Occur?" Seek to comprehend the reasons for the issue so you can guarantee that it doesn't occur once more. If an issue repeats in your life or business, it is an indication that your business is inadequately composed or wild around there. There is a deformity incorporated with your frameworks that is making a similar issue repeat. Your responsibility is to discover why this happens repeatedly so you can take care of the issue at its root.

Stage 5: Ask,

"What Are All the Possible Solutions?" The more potential arrangements you create, the almost certain you will think of the correct one.

The nature of the arrangement is by all accounts in a direct extent to the number of arrangements considered in critical thinking. Be careful with an issue for which there is just a single arrangement.

Stage 6: Ask,

"What Is the Best Solution right now?" Sometimes, any arrangement is superior to no arrangement. A normal arrangement overwhelmingly executed is frequently better than an astounding arrangement that can't be actualized on account of its multifaceted nature or because nobody can execute it. The standard is that completely 80 percent of all issues ought to be managed right away. Just 20 percent of issues should be put off to a later time. If you should put off an issue, set a particular cutoff time for settling on a choice on that issue, and afterward settle on your choice at that cutoff time with whatever data you have around then. There is a standard that says that each enormous issue was at one time a little issue that could have been explained effectively and modestly around then. Once in a while, the best methodology is to "halt it from the beginning." When there is an issue and an answer, do what must be done — and do it rapidly.

Stage 7: Make a Decision. Select an answer, any arrangement, and afterward settle on a game-plan. Continuously ask, "What is our next activity? What are we going to do now?"

Stage 8: Assign Responsibility. Who precisely is going to arrange the various components of the arrangement? It is very regular for a gathering to meet to take care of an issue and concur on an answer, yet when the gathering meets again two weeks after the fact, nothing has occurred incidentally. Why? Nobody was made explicitly answerable for completing the choice.

Stage 9: Set a Measure for the Decision. What are you attempting to achieve with this choice, and by what method will you measure results? In what capacity will you realize that it worked? The more precisely you can decide the outcome that you need to accomplish by the arrangement, the more probable it is to accomplish it.

The Determinant of Your Success

In your work, your critical thinking capacity generally decides all that you achieve. Individuals who are acceptable at taking care of issues are the absolute generally significant and regarded individuals in each territory. Hence, achievement has been characterized as "the capacity to take care of issues." This additionally implies satisfaction is the capacity to take care of issues. The administration is the capacity to take care of issues. At the point when you practice self-control and poise in the face of the inescapable and unavoidable issues and emergencies of everyday life, you become progressively skillful and viable in all that you do. You will be regarded and regarded by everybody around you. You will encounter a huge sentiment of individual force and ability. In a matter of moments by any stretch of the imagination, you will get one of the most significant individuals in your association.

As per protection industry insights, of one hundred individuals who start work at age twenty-one, by age sixty-five, one will be rich, four will be financially autonomous, fifteen will have some cash set aside, and the other eighty will be as yet working, broke, subject to benefits, or dead. Most children of post-war America today are wanting to work into their seventies. Why would that be? It is because they need more cash set aside so they can quit working.

The essential explanation behind monetary issues in life is the absence of self-control, self-dominance, and self-control. It is the failure to postpone delight for the time being.

It is the propensity for individuals to spend all that they win and somewhat more moreover, for the most part, enhanced by advances and charge card obligations. Today, the reserve funds rate in America is too low to even consider achieving monetary freedom. After a lifetime of work, the normal American family has total assets of just about $8,000. Individuals proceed to spend and obtain consequences be damned. Fortunately, we are living in the most well-off time in all of mankind's history. There are more chances to accomplish riches and thriving today for additional individuals. In more unexpected manners in comparison to have at any point existed throughout the entire existence of man. It has never been progressively feasible for you to accomplish budgetary autonomy than the present moment. Be that as it may, you should make a goal to do it, and afterward, you should finish on your goals.

Chapter 21: The Reasons For Financial Failure

The essential motivation behind why most grown-ups have budgetary issues can't profit. In their book, The Millionaire Next Door, Thomas Stanley and William Danko show that two families living on a similar road, in a similar size of a house, and working at a similar activity can have great money related circumstances. By the age of forty-five or fifty, the couple in one house will be monetarily free. The couple nearby is profoundly in a difficult situation making the base installments on their Mastercards.

The explanation behind this can't measure of cash that they acquire. The explanation is the absence of self-control and the failure to postpone satisfaction. For what reason is this shortcoming of character so pervasive among most grown-ups in the public arena today? It returns to youth. At the point when you were a youngster, and you got cash (regardless of whether it was your remittance or a blessing from a companion or relative), the principal thing you thought of doing was to spend that cash on sweets. Candy is sweet. Candy is tasty. Candy fills your mouth with a superb, sugary flavor. You preferred sweets when you were a kid, and you presumably could only get enough of it from time to time. Numerous youngsters will eat candy until they become truly sick since it tastes so great. As you developed more established, you created what therapists call an "adapted reaction" to accepting cash from any source. Like Pavlov's canine, when you get cash, you intellectually salivate at the idea of spending this cash on something that fulfills you in any event briefly.

Spending Makes You Happy

When you become a grown-up and gain or get cash, this programmed response proceeds. Your first idea is, "How might I go through this cash to accomplish quick joy?" When you land your first position, the absolute first thing you consider is how you can go through the cash you gain. Yet, additionally, every penny you can acquire on a Visa on garments, vehicles, beauty care products, mingling, diversion, travel, and everything else. Your psychological condition is cash = delight. At the point when you travel to a retreat of any sort, you find that the lodgings and lanes are fixed with shops selling futile knickknacks, bobbles, and garbage, in addition to garments, fine art, and different things that you could never consider purchasing at home. Why would that be? Basic. At the point when you are in the midst of a get-away, you feel cheerful. You have an adapted reaction to connect satisfaction with going through cash. The more joyful you are, the more unwittingly constrained you are to go out and burn through cash on something — or, instead, on anything. It is very regular for some individuals to go out on the town to shop when they are despondent or baffled in any way, shape, or form. They unwittingly partner purchasing something with being upbeat. At the point when it doesn't function as they expected, they are buying something different. Once in awhile, despondent individuals continue shopping binges. They purchase loads of things they don't especially require because they unknowingly partner going through with satisfaction.

As an adult, whenever you get a check, reward, commission, the first thing you absolutely must consider is how to use this cash as quickly as you can, but in the many joys that can be allowed.

Your Responses About Money

The beginning stage of accomplishing monetary freedom is to teach yourself to rework your mentality toward cash. You have to venture into your intuitive psyche and disengage the wire connecting "spending" and "bliss." You have to then reconnect that "joy" wire to the "sparing and contributing" wire. From that minute on, rather than saying, "I feel glad when I go through cash," you will say, "I feel upbeat when I set aside cash."

To fortify this move-in speculation, open up a "monetary opportunity account" at your nearby bank. This is the record wherein you store cash as long as possible. When your cash goes into this record, you settle that you will never spend it on anything besides accomplishing money-related opportunities. If you need to set aside cash to purchase a vessel or a vehicle, you open up a different record exclusively for that reason. In any case, your budgetary opportunity account is sacred. You never contact it but to contribute those assets with the goal that they can yield a higher pace of return.

Partner Happiness with Saving

At the point when you start sparing right now, phenomenal occurs inside you. You begin to feel cheerful about having cash in the bank. Regardless of whether you open your record with just $10, this activity gives you a sentiment of more considerable restraint and individual force. You feel more joyful about yourself. The very demonstration of teaching yourself to set aside cash causes you to feel more grounded and more in charge of your fate.

Each time you get some additional cash, you put it into your budgetary opportunity account. In the end, your budgetary opportunity record will start to develop. At that point, as it develops, you initiate two laws: the Law of Attraction and the Law of Accumulation.

Since your musings and sentiments emotionalize the cash in your record, it sets up a power field of vitality that starts to draw in more cash into it. On the off chance that you spare $10 per month for a year, you will be dumbfounded to find that with the additional bits of cash that you have placed into that account, you will likely have more than $200 as opposed to simply $120. On the off chance that you spare $100 every month, you will presumably have more than $2,000.

The Law of Accumulation says that "each incredible accomplishment is a gathering of numerous little accomplishments." The Law of Attraction says that "you pull in into your life those things that are incongruity with your prevailing musings." Because of these laws, your budgetary opportunity account starts to develop with the marvel of compound interest. The more cash you have in your ledger, the more vitality it produces, and the more cash are pulled into your life. You have heard it said that "it takes cash to bring in cash." This is valid. As you set aside and gather cash, the universe starts to coordinate more cash increasingly toward you that you can spare and collect. Everybody who has ever rehearsed this customary sparing guideline is completely amazed at how rapidly their budgetary fortunes improve.

When you have overhauled your mentality toward cash, the standard for budgetary freedom is to "pay yourself first." Most individuals spare anything that remains over their month to month costs if anything is left over. As it may, the key is to pay yourself first, off the top, from each measure of cash you get.

Conclusion

Self-discipline, which I consider an incredible quality isn't regular; it is something that you or any other individual can create and improve after some time. It resembles heading off to the rec center or getting into some sportive action, much like a muscle getting more grounded by being utilized and prepared.

However, you have to recollect that it isn't just about the abilities you improve, yet also about the moves you make in your life. To be a self-disciplined mind, you must be prepared and ready to face whatever challenges are required to carry out the job.

It implies that you ought to never be hiding in the back of the class, yet instead, get in front to push ahead until you achieve your aim.

To develop self-discipline, you have to remain on course. Remember your objectives. Realize that the greatest enemy to arrive at your wants is consistently the easy way out. If you pick the cover-up street, what is important, however, perhaps hard, you will never understand the objectives, achievement, or satisfaction you are capable of accomplishing in your life.

Luckily, you can build up the habit of self-discipline. The ordinary act of teaching yourself to do what you ought to do when you ought to do it, regardless of whether you feel like it or not, gets more grounded and more grounded as you practice it. You won't rationalize.

Bad habits are easy to form, however difficult to live with. Great habits are difficult to shape yet simple to live with. And as Goethe stated, "Everything is difficult before it's simple."

It is hard to form the habits of self-discipline, self-mastery, and self-control, but once you have developed them, they become automatic and easy to practice. When self-discipline habits are firmly entrenched in your behavior, you start to feel uncomfortable when you do not behave in a self-disciplined manner.

It is difficult to frame self-discipline habits, self-mastery, and self-control; however, once you have developed them, they become programmed and straightforward to rehearse. When self-discipline habits are firmly entrenched in your behavior, you begin to feel awkward when you do not carry on in a self-disciplined manner.

The best news is that all habits are learnable. You can get familiar with any habit to learn to turn into the sort of individual you need to turn into. You can turn into a superb individual by rehearsing self-discipline whenever it is called for. The practice of self-discipline strengthens every other discipline. Tragically, every shortcoming in discipline weakens your other disciplines as well.

To build up the habit of self-discipline, you first make a firm choice about how you will carry on in a specific area of activity. At that point, you won't permit exemptions until the habit of self- in that area is firmly established. Each time you slip, as you will, you resolve once again to keep rehearsing self-discipline until it gets simpler for you to act in a disciplined manner than to carry on in a disorderly manner.